Modern Critical Interpretations

Henry James's
Daisy Miller, The Turn of the Screw, and Other Tales

Bloom's Modern Critical Interpretations

Adventures of
    Huckleberry Finn
All Quiet on the
    Western Front
Animal Farm
Beloved
Beowulf
Billy Budd, Benito
    Cereno, Bartleby
    the Scrivener, and
    Other Tales
The Bluest Eye
Brave New World
Cat on a Hot Tin Roof
The Catcher in the Rye
Catch-22
Cat's Cradle
The Color Purple
Crime and
    Punishment
The Crucible
Daisy Miller, The
    Turn of the Screw,
    and Other Tales
David Copperfield
Death of a Salesman
The Divine Comedy
Don Quixote
Dracula
Dubliners
Emma
Fahrenheit 451
A Farewell to Arms
Frankenstein
The General Prologue
    to the Canterbury
    Tales
The Glass Menagerie
The Grapes of Wrath
Great Expectations
The Great Gatsby
Gulliver's Travels

Hamlet
The Handmaid's Tale
Heart of Darkness
I Know Why the
    Caged Bird Sings
The Iliad
The Interpretation of
    Dreams
Invisible Man
Jane Eyre
The Joy Luck Club
Julius Caesar
The Jungle
King Lear
Long Day's Journey
    Into Night
Lord of the Flies
The Lord of the Rings
Macbeth
The Merchant of Venice
The Metamorphosis
A Midsummer Night's
    Dream
Moby-Dick
My Ántonia
Native Son
Night
1984
The Odyssey
Oedipus Rex
The Old Man and
    the Sea
One Flew Over the
    Cuckoo's Nest
One Hundred Years
    of Solitude
Othello
Paradise Lost
The Pardoner's Tale
A Portrait of the Artist
    as a Young Man
Pride and Prejudice

Ragtime
The Red Badge
    of Courage
The Rime of the
    Ancient Mariner
Romeo & Juliet
The Scarlet Letter
A Scholarly Look at
    The Diary of
    Anne Frank
A Separate Peace
Silas Marner
Slaughterhouse-Five
Song of Myself
Song of Solomon
The Sonnets of
    William Shakespeare
Sophie's Choice
The Sound and
    the Fury
The Stranger
A Streetcar Named
    Desire
Sula
The Sun Also Rises
A Tale of Two Cities
The Tales of Poe
The Tempest
Tess of the
    D'Urbervilles
Their Eyes Were
    Watching God
Things Fall Apart
To Kill a Mockingbird
Waiting for Godot
Walden
The Waste Land
White Noise
Wuthering Heights

Modern Critical Interpretations

Henry James's
Daisy Miller, The Turn of the Screw,
and Other Tales

Edited and with an introduction by

Harold Bloom
Sterling Professor of the Humanities
Yale University

Chelsea House Publishers

PHILADELPHIA

10   9   8   7   6

The Chelsea House World Wide Web address is
http://www.chelseahouse.com

∞ The paper used in this publication meets the minimum
requirements of the American National Standard for
Permanence of Paper for Printed Library Materials,
Z39.48–1984.

Library of Congress Cataloging-in-Publication Data
Henry James's Daisy Miller, The turn of the screw,
    and other tales.
    (Modern critical interpretations)
    Bibliography: p.
    Includes index.
    Summary: A collection of eight critical essays on
the major novellas of James including "The Aspern
Papers," "Daisy Miller," and "The Turn of the Screw."
    1. James, Henry, 1843–1916—Criticism and
interpretation.   [1. James, Henry, 1843–1916—Criticism
and interpretation.   2. American literature—History
and criticism]   I. Bloom, Harold.   II. Series.
PS2124.H48   1987   813'.4   87-5215
ISBN 1-55546-007-0

Contents

Editor's Note / vii

Introduction / 1
    HAROLD BLOOM

"The Aspern Papers" / 11
    LAURENCE HOLLAND

"Daisy Miller": A Study of Changing Intentions / 25
    CAROL OHMANN

Partial Art—Total Interpretation / 35
    WOLFGANG ISER

A Reading of "The Real Thing" / 43
    MOSHE RON

"The Figure in the Carpet" / 61
    J. HILLIS MILLER

A Jamesian About-Face: Notes on "The Jolly Corner" / 75
    DEBORAH ESCH

The "Lost Stuff of Consciousness": The Priority of Futurity
and the Deferral of Desire in "The Beast in the Jungle" / 93
    DONNA PRZYBYLOWICZ

"Hanging Fire": The Primal Scene of
The Turn of the Screw / 117
    NED LUKACHER

Chronology / 133

Contributors / 135

Bibliography / 137

Acknowledgments / 141

Index / 143

Editor's Note

This book brings together a representative selection of the best criticism devoted to seven of the major novellas of Henry James: "The Aspern Papers," "Daisy Miller," "The Figure in the Carpet," "The Real Thing," "The Jolly Corner," "The Beast in the Jungle," and *The Turn of the Screw*. The critical essays are reprinted here in the chronological order of their original publication. I am grateful to Thomas Keenan for his aid in editing this volume.

My introduction first centers upon the complex fate of James's relation to Emerson. The chronological sequence of criticism begins with Laurence Holland's reading of "The Aspern Papers," which gives equal emphasis to "both the comedy and horror of the tale."

Carol Ohmann, studying "Daisy Miller," finds in it "a work that shows unmistakable signs of shifting authorial intention and attitude." The major theorist of "reader response" criticism, Wolfgang Iser, employs "The Figure in the Carpet" as an instance of James's dubiety as to the value of a search for meaning in narrative. Deconstructing "The Real Thing" in the mode of the late Paul de Man, Moshe Ron examines the ways in which the story works to subvert its own authority.

J. Hillis Miller, in the second of this book's analyses of "The Figure in the Carpet," uncovers in the tale a struggle between the author as father and the author as son. In a related account, Deborah Esch studies the dialectical weavings of "The Jolly Corner" and comes to rest upon an element in the story that is beyond anyone's influence, whether character, narrator, or reader.

"The Beast in the Jungle," a great parable of the unlived life, is read by Donna Przybylowicz as a vision of future emptiness and a search for lost potential in past and present. In this book's final essay, Ned Lukacher centers on the Primal Scene of *The Turn of the Screw* and examines the novella's parallels to Freudian mechanisms of repression.

Introduction

The intense critical admirers of Henry James go so far as to call him the major American writer, or even the most accomplished novelist in the English language. The first assertion neglects only Walt Whitman, while the second partly evades the marvelous sequence that moves from Samuel Richardson's *Clarissa* through Jane Austen on to George Eliot, and the alternative tradition that goes from Fielding through Dickens to Joyce. James is certainly the crucial American novelist, and in his best works the true peer of Austen and George Eliot. His precursor, Hawthorne, is more than fulfilled in the splendors of *The Portrait of a Lady* and *The Wings of the Dove*, giant descendants of *The Marble Faun*, while the rival American novelists—Melville, Mark Twain, Dreiser, Faulkner—survive comparison with James only by being so totally unlike him. Unlikeness makes Faulkner—particularly in his great phase—a true if momentary rival, and perhaps if you are to find a non-Jamesian sense of sustained power in the American novel, you need to seek out our curious antithetical tradition that moves between *Moby-Dick* and its darker descendants: *As I Lay Dying*, *Miss Lonelyhearts*, *The Crying of Lot 49*. The normative consciousness of our prose fiction, first prophesied by *The Scarlet Letter*, was forged by Henry James, whose spirit lingers not only in palpable disciples like Edith Wharton in *The Age of Innocence* and Willa Cather in her superb *A Lost Lady*, but more subtly (because merged with Joseph Conrad's aura) in novelists as various as Fitzgerald, Hemingway, and Warren. It seems clear that the relation of James to American prose fiction is precisely analogous to Whitman's relation to our poetry; each is, in his own sphere, what Emerson prophesied as the Central Man who would come and change all things forever, in a celebration of the American Newness.

The irony of James's central position among our novelists is palpable, since, like the much smaller figure of T. S. Eliot later on, James abandoned

1

his nation and eventually became a British subject, after having been born a citizen in Emerson's America. But it is a useful commonplace of criticism that James remained the most American of novelists, not less peculiarly nationalistic in *The Ambassadors* than he had been in "Daisy Miller" and *The American*. James, a subtle if at times perverse literary critic, understood very well what we continue to learn and relearn; an American writer can be Emersonian or anti-Emersonian, but even a negative stance towards Emerson always leads back again to his formulation of the post-Christian American religion of Self-Reliance. Overt Emersonians like Thoreau, Whitman, and Frost are no more pervaded by the Sage of Concord than are anti-Emersonians like Hawthorne, Melville, and Eliot. Perhaps the most haunted are those writers who evade Emerson, yet never leave his dialectical ambiance, a group that includes Emily Dickinson, Henry James, and Wallace Stevens.

Emerson was for Henry James something of a family tradition, though that in itself hardly accounts for the plain failure of very nearly everything that the novelist wrote about the essayist. James invariably resorts to a tone of ironic indulgence on the subject of Emerson, which is hardly appropriate to the American prophet of Power, Fate, Illusions, and Wealth. I suggest that James unknowingly mixed Emerson up with the sage's good friend Henry James, Sr., whom we dismiss as a Swedenborgian, but who might better be characterized as an American Gnostic speculator, in Emerson's mode, though closer in eminence to, say, Bronson Alcott than to the author of *The Conduct of Life*.

The sane and sacred Emerson was a master of evasions, particularly when disciples became too pressing, whether upon personal or spiritual matters. The senior Henry James is remembered now for having fathered Henry, William, and Alice, and also for his famous outburst against Emerson, whom he admired on the other side of idolatry: "O you man without a handle!"

The junior Henry James, overtly celebrating Emerson, nevertheless remarked: "It is hardly too much, or too little, to say of Emerson's writings in general that they were not composed at all." "Composed" is the crucial word there, and makes me remember a beautiful moment in Stevens's "The Poems of Our Climate":

> There would still remain the never-resting mind,
> So that one would want to escape, come back
> To what had been so long composed.

Emerson's mind, never merely restless, indeed was never-resting, as was the mind of every member of the James family. The writings of Emerson, not composed at all, constantly come back to what had been so long composed, to what his admirer Nietzsche called the primordial poem of mankind, the fiction that we have knocked together and called our cosmos. James was far too subtle not to have known this. He chose not to know it, because he needed a provincial Emerson even as he needed a provincial Hawthorne, just as he needed a New England that never was: simple, gentle, and isolated, even a little childlike.

The days when T. S. Eliot could wonder why Henry James had not carved up R. W. Emerson seem safely past, but we ought to remember Eliot's odd complaint about James as critic: "Even in handling men whom he could, one supposes, have carved joint from joint—Emerson or Norton —his touch is uncertain; there is a desire to be generous, a political motive, an admission (in dealing with American writers) that under the circumstances this was the best possible, or that it has fine qualities." Aside from appearing to rank Emerson with Charles Eliot Norton (which is comparable to ranking Freud with Bernard Berenson), this unamiable judgment reduces Emerson, who was and is merely the mind of America, to the stature of a figure who might, at most, warrant the condescension of James (and of Eliot). The cultural polemic involved is obvious, and indeed obsessive, in Eliot, but though pleasanter in James is really no more acceptable:

Of the three periods into which his life divides itself, the first was (as in the case of most men) that of movement, experiment and selection—that of effort too and painful probation. Emerson had his message, but he was a good while looking for his form—the form which, as he himself would have said, he never completely found and of which it was rather characteristic of him that his later years (with their growing refusal to give him the *word*), wishing to attack him in his most vulnerable point, where his tenure was least complete, had in some degree the effect of despoiling him. It all sounds rather bare and stern, Mr. Cabot's account of his youth and early manhood, and we get an impression of a terrible paucity of alternatives. If he would be neither a farmer nor a trader he could "teach school"; that was the main resource and a part of the general educative process of the young New Englander who proposed to devote himself to the things of the mind. There was an advantage in the nudity, however, which was that, in Emerson's case at least, the things of the mind did get themselves admirably well considered. If it be his great distinction and his special sign that he had a more vivid conception of the moral life than any one else, it is probably not fanciful to say that he owed it in part to the limited way in which he saw our capacity for living illustrated. The plain, God-fearing, practical society which surrounded him was not fertile in variations: it had great intelligence and energy, but it moved altogether in the straightforward direction. On three occasions later—three journeys to Europe—he was introduced to a more complicated world; but his spirit, his moral taste, as it were, abode always within the undecorated walls of his youth. There he could dwell with that ripe unconsciousness of evil which is one of the most beautiful signs by which we know him. His early writings are full of quaint animadversion upon the vices of the place and time, but there is something charmingly vague, light and general in the arraignment. Almost the worst he can say is that these vices are negative and that his fellow-townsmen are not heroic. We feel that his first impressions were gathered in a community from which misery and extravagance, and either extreme, of any sort, were equally absent. What the life of New England fifty years ago offered to the observer was the common lot, in a kind of achromatic picture, without particular intensifications. It was from this table of the usual, the merely typical joys and sorrows that he proceeded to generalise—a fact that accounts in some degree for a certain inadequacy and thinness in his enumerations. But it helps to account also for his direct, intimate vision of the soul itself—not in its emotions, its contortions and perversions, but in its passive, exposed, yet healthy form. He knows the nature of man and the long tradition of its dangers; but we feel that whereas he can put his finger on the remedies, lying for the most part, as they do, in the deep recesses of virtue, of the spirit, he has only a kind of hearsay, uninformed acquaintance with the disorders. It would require some ingenuity, the reader may say too much, to trace closely this correspondence between his genius and the frugal, dutiful, happy but decidedly lean Boston of the past, where there was a great deal of will but very little fulcrum—like a ministry without an opposition.

The genius itself it seems to me impossible to contest—I mean the genius for seeing character as a real and supreme thing. Other writers have arrived at a more complete expression: Wordsworth and Goethe, for instance, give one a sense of having found their form, whereas with Emerson we never lose the sense that he is still seeking it. But no one has had so steady and constant, and above all so natural, a vision of what we require and what we are capable of in the way of aspiration and independence. With Emerson it is ever the special capacity for moral experience —always that and only that. We have the impression, somehow, that life had never bribed him to look at anything but the soul; and indeed in the world in which he grew up and lived the bribes and lures, the beguilements and prizes, were few. He was in an admirable position for showing, what he constantly endeavoured to show, that the prize was within. Any one who in New England at that time could do that was sure of success, of listeners and sympathy: most of all, of course, when it was a question of doing it with such a divine persuasiveness. Moreover, the way in which Emerson did it added to the charm—by word of mouth, face to face, with a rare, irresistible voice and a beautiful mild, modest authority. If Mr. Arnold is struck with the limited degree in which he was a man of letters I suppose it is because he is more struck with his having been, as it were, a man of lectures. But the lecture surely was never more purged of its grossness—the quality in it that suggests a strong light and a big brush—than as it issued from Emerson's lips; so far from being a vulgarisation, it was simply the esoteric made audible, and instead of treating the few as the many, after the usual fashion of gentlemen on platforms, he treated the many as the few. There was probably no other society at that time in which he would have got so many persons to understand that; for we think the better of his audience as we read him, and wonder where else people would have had so much moral attention to give. It is to be remembered however that during the winter of 1847–48, on the occasion of his second visit to England, he found many listeners in London and in provincial cities. Mr. Cabot's volumes are full of evidence of the satisfactions he offered, the delights and revelations he may be said to have promised, to a race which had to seek its entertainment, its rewards and consolations, almost exclusively in the moral world. But his own writings are fuller still; we find an instance almost wherever we open them.

It is astonishing to me that James judged Emerson's "great distinction" and "special sign" to be "that he had a more vivid conception of the moral life than anyone else," unless "the moral life" has an altogether Jamesian meaning. I would rather say that the great distinction and special sign of James's fiction is that it represents a more vivid conception of the moral life than even Jane Austen or George Eliot could convey to us. Emerson is not much more concerned with morals than he is with manners; his subjects are power, freedom, and fate. As for "that ripe unconsciousness of evil" that James found in Emerson, I have not been able to find it myself, after reading Emerson almost daily for the last twenty years, and I am reminded of Yeats's late essay on Shelley's *Prometheus Unbound*, in which Yeats declares that his skeptical and passionate precursor, great poet that he certainly was, necessarily lacked the Vision of Evil. The necessity in both strong misreadings, James's and Yeats's, was to clear more space for themselves.

Jealous as I am for Emerson, I can recognize that no critic has matched James in seeing and saying what Emerson's strongest virtue is: "But no one has had so steady and constant, and above all so natural, a vision of what we require and what we are capable of in the way of aspiration and independence." No one, that is, except Henry James, for that surely is the quest of Isabel Archer towards her own quite Emersonian vision of aspiration and independence. "The moral world" is James's phrase and James's emphasis. Emerson's own emphasis, I suspect, was considerably more pragmatic than that of James. When James returned to America in 1904 on a visit, after twenty years of self-exile, he went back to Concord and recorded his impressions in *The American Scene*:

> It is odd, and it is also exquisite, that these witnessing ways should be the last ground on which we feel moved to ponderation of the "Concord school"—to use, I admit, a futile expression; or rather, I should doubtless say, it *would* be odd if there were not inevitably something absolute in the fact of Emerson's all but lifelong connection with them. We may smile a little as we "drag in" Weimar, but I confess myself, for my part, much more satisfied than not by our happy equivalent, "in American money," for Goethe and Schiller. The money is a potful in the second case as in the first, and if Goethe, in the one, represents the gold and Schiller the silver, I find (and quite putting aside any bimetallic prejudice) the same good relation in the other between Emerson and Thoreau. I open Emerson for the same benefit for which I open Goethe, the sense of moving in large intellectual space, and that of the gush, here and there, out of the rock, of the crystalline cupful, in wisdom and poetry, in Wahrheit and Dichtung; and whatever I open Thoreau for (I

needn't take space here for the good reasons) I open him oftener than I open Schiller. Which comes back to our feeling that the rarity of Emerson's genius, which has made him so, for the attentive peoples, the first, and the one really rare, American spirit in letters, couldn't have spent his career in a charming woody, watery place, for so long socially and typically and, above all, interestingly homogeneous, without an effect as of the communication to it of something ineffaceable. It was during his long span his immediate concrete, sufficient world; it gave him his nearest vision of life, and he drew half his images, we recognize, from the revolution of its seasons and the play of its manners. I don't speak of the other half, which he drew from elsewhere. It is admirably, to-day, as if we were still seeing these things *in* those images, which stir the air like birds, dim in the eventide, coming home to nest. If one had reached a "time of life" one had thereby at least heard him lecture; and not a russet leaf fell for me, while I was there, but fell with an Emersonian drop.

That is a beautiful study of the nostalgias and tells us, *contra* T. S. Eliot, what James's relation to Emerson actually was. We know how much that is essential in William James was quarried out of Emerson, particularly from the essay "Experience," which gave birth to Pragmatism. Henry James was not less indebted to Emerson than William James was. *The Portrait of a Lady* is hardly an Emersonian novel; perhaps *The Scarlet Letter* actually is closer to that. Yet Isabel Archer is Emerson's daughter, just as Lambert Strether is Emerson's heir. The Emersonian aura also lingers on even in the ghostly tales of Henry James.

II

My own favorite among James's nouvelles is "The Pupil" (1891), not a ghostly tale, yet still deeply (if dialectically) Emersonian. "The Pupil" comes between the culmination of the earlier James in *The Bostonians* and *The Princess Casamassima* (both 1886) and the middle James of *The Spoils of Poynton* and *What Maisie Knew* (both 1897), and *The Awkward Age* (1899). In some respects, "The Pupil" seems to me the perfection in shorter form of James's earlier mode even as *The Portrait of a Lady* is its perfection on a full scale. Yet "The Pupil" is an enigmatic tale, so nuanced that a single interpretation is unlikely ever to gain wide credence.

In his "Preface to the New York Edition," James is suitably remote on the actual moral drama enacted in "The Pupil." Writing on *What Maisie Knew*, James remarks that: "Small children have many more perceptions than they have terms to translate them; their vision is at any moment much richer, their apprehension even constantly stronger, than their prompt, their at all producible, vocabulary." Among Jamesian children, the tragic Morgan is the great exception to this principle; his preternaturally formidable vocabulary is invariably at the service of his accurate and comprehensive perceptions. Of Morgan, James affectionately observes: "My urchin of 'The Pupil' has sensibility in abundance; it would seem—and yet preserves in spite of it, I judge, his strong little male quality." It is certainly part of the story's immense charm that all of us, very quickly, come to share the author's (and Pemberton's) affection for Morgan, who is one of the grand portraits of the American as a young boy. I can think of no two American novelists of real eminence who shared as little as Henry James and Mark Twain, and yet I could imagine a conversation between Morgan Moreen and Huck Finn, two very different yet complementary images of the American boy longing for freedom.

In the only reference to Twain I can recall in James, the master rather nastily remarks (in 1874), that: "In the day of Mark Twain there is no harm in being reminded that the absence of drollery may, at a stretch, be compensated by the presence of sublimity." Well, James said far worse about Whitman and Dickens, and I myself prefer *Adventures of Huckleberry Finn* even to *The Portrait of a Lady*, but if we strip from James's observation its apotropaic gesture, we can grant that "The Pupil" abounds both in drollery and sublimity, even though clearly inferior to *Huckleberry Finn* in both qualities. Poor Morgan, very much a changeling in the Moreen family, would have benefited more even from Huck Finn as tutor than from Pemberton, if only Morgan had been robust enough to bear it.

There has been a critical fashion to blame the long-suffering and devoted Pemberton, as well as the outrageous Moreens, for Morgan's death, but this seems to me merely absurd. What after all could the penniless Pemberton, barely self-supporting even when free of the Moreens, have done with Morgan? The novella's final scene is exquisitely subtle, yet in my reading contains no abandonment of Morgan by Pemberton:

> "We've struggled, we've suffered," his wife went on; "but you've made him so your own that we've already been through the worst of the sacrifice."
> Morgan had turned away from his father—he stood looking at Pemberton with a light in his face. His sense of shame for

their common humiliated state had dropped; the case had another side —the thing was to clutch at *that*. He had a moment of boyish joy, scarcely mitigated by the reflexion that with this unexpected consecration of his hope —too sudden and too violent; the turn taken was away from a *good* boy's book—the "escape" was left on their hands. The boyish joy was there an instant, and Pemberton was almost scared at the rush of gratitude and affection that broke through his first abasement. When he stammered "My dear fellow, what do you say to *that*?" how could one not say something enthusiastic? But there was more need for courage at something else that immediately followed and that made the lad sit down quickly on the nearest chair. He had turned quite livid and had raised his hand to his left side. They were all three looking at him, but Mrs. Moreen suddenly bounded forward. "Ah his darling little heart!" she broke out; and this time, on her knees before him and without respect for the idol, she caught him ardently in her arms. "You walked him too far, you hurried him too fast!" she hurled over her shoulder at Pemberton. Her son made no protest, and the next instant, still holding him, she sprang up with her face convulsed and with the terrified cry "Help, help! he's going, he's gone!" Pemberton saw with equal horror, by Morgan's own stricken face, that he was beyond their wildest recall. He pulled him half out of his mother's hands, and for a moment, while they held him together, they looked all their dismay into each other's eyes. "He couldn't stand it with his weak organ," said Pemberton— "the shock, the whole scene, the violent emotion."

"But I thought he *wanted* to go to you!" wailed Mrs. Moreen.

"I *told* you he didn't, my dear," her husband made answer. Mr. Moreen was trembling all over and was in his way as deeply affected as his wife. But after the very first he took his bereavement as a man of the world.

Morgan, as I read it, dies not of grief at rejection, whether by the Moreens or Pemberton, but of excess of joy at the prospect of being taken away by Pemberton. This seems to me strikingly similar to the death of King Lear, since I agree with Harold Goddard's interpretation that Lear dies of joy rather than grief, in the hallucinated conviction that Cordelia's lips still move. What Yeats called "tragic joy" is a Shakespearean quality not easy to achieve, and it is extraordinary that James attains to that vision at the close of "The Pupil." But that still leaves us with the moral question concerning this great fiction; what could there have been for Morgan in a world so clearly inadequate to him?

James's beautiful (and false) objection to our father Emerson was that the sage had failed to achieve a style, and had to survive "on the strength of his message alone." I am hardly among those who find Emerson's message to be weak, but I know it to be strong primarily through and by his style. Wisdom has no authority for us unless and until it has individualized its rhetorical stance, and what preserves Emerson's shamanistic charisma is precisely his style. I find a touch, slight but definite, of that style in "The Pupil" which is nothing but an Emersonian parable of the fate of freedom or wildness in an alien context, which is to say, of the tragedy of the American spirit when it is taken into exile abroad, into the social perversions and false values of the Old World. James will not say so, in his "Preface," but Morgan is a victim of Europe, and of his family's vain attempt to domesticate itself in a realm where the Adamic stance has no proper place.

Read thus, "The Pupil" indeed becomes a sublime drollery, distant but authentic cousin to *Adventures of Huckleberry Finn.* Henry James, who finally became a subject of King George V, could not tolerate that admirable American writer, Mark Twain, who once deliciously suggested that the British ought to replace the House of Hanover by a medley of royal cats and kittens. But that did not prevent James from writing an involuntary self-chastisement in "The Pupil," an eloquent reprise of the Emersonian warning of the American fate if we did not face west into the evening-land, abandoning behind us the false dream of becoming men and women of the European world.

"The Aspern Papers"

Laurence Holland

Both the comedy and horror of the tale are sustained by the paradoxically double perspective which is created for the reader by the Scoundrel's first efforts, with the help of his friend Mrs. Prest, to launch his " 'plot,' " as it is called, his " 'kind of conspiracy.' " One perspective is that of utterly bland yet bold candor which is the Editor's unabashed manner with Mrs. Prest and through her with the reader. The other is that of cagey duplicity, exercised at first with Juliana and Miss Tina and through them with the reader as well, the reader being prevented by the Narrator from knowing even the alias which he uses, let alone his real name, which he manages to divulge later to Tina without giving the reader even his initials. In such close and unremitting proximity are the candor and the duplicity that each becomes outlandish, and they are ludicrous and starkly shocking both in the bold contrast they afford and in the fantastic oddity of their conjunction.

When the Scoundrel announces to Mrs. Prest that " 'Hypocrisy, duplicity are my only chance,' " and when he opens the second chapter with the transparently Satanic declaration " 'I must work the garden—I must work the garden,' " he is rehearsing a fraud before our eyes: acknowledging it nakedly while beginning to practice it, naming his role while playing it, confessing his artful disguise while donning it. Part of the somber comedy inheres in the fact that his conduct never loses this quality of a rehearsal even when he begins the performance of his plan and moves closer to its achievement. Whatever may have been his motives and reactions originally

From *The Expense of Vision: Essays on the Craft of Henry James.* © 1964 by Faith Holland.

(we have access only to the "introducer" of the experience and cannot confront him with his former self), the recollection which he begins to gather in his narrative is colored by his knowing in advance the main outlines of all he discovered and underwent in his negotiations with the Misses Bordereau. When he recalls that "I was beating about the bush, trying to be ingenious, wondering by what combination of arts I might become an acquaintance [of the Bordereaus]," he displays not only the anticipations of an unscrupulous historian and opportunist but also the tone of a bemused spectator, after the fact, of his own conceit and futility.

A different attitude, anxious and disturbed, is revealed in fusion with these by the time he has finished the first paragraph. He declares that the decisively "fruitful idea in the whole business"—that "the way to become an acquaintance was first to become an intimate"—was Mrs. Prest's clever contribution to his scheme, and he shortly recalls that Mrs. Prest had once offered help to the Bordereaus when old Juliana was sick so as not to have the guilt of neglect "on her conscience." The moral implications of these remarks are complicated when the Editor recalls "laying siege . . . with my eyes" to Juliana's "citadel" and feeling that the sound of Jeffrey Aspern's "voice seemed to abide there by a roundabout implication and in a 'dying fall.' " In these remarks are embedded the waking nightmare which is the Editor's stunned recognition not only of his own lurid deeds but of a collaboration, in which his partners include Mrs. Prest (the helpful onlooker, eager for amusement) and the poet Aspern himself.

Mrs. Prest's patience is limited—to the Publisher's relief, she leaves Venice in June, having "expected to draw amusement from the drama of my intercourse with the Misses Bordereau" but being "disappointed that the intercourse, and consequently the drama, had not come off." She had for weeks "reproached me for lacking boldness" and for "wasting precious hours in whimpering in her salon," for, while she "hadn't the nerves of an editor," my "eagerness amused her" and she relished my "fine case of monomania." The tale's horror derives partly from the fact that Mrs. Prest, fruitful idea and all, defines not only her own but the reader's engagement with the Scoundrel's project: the reader's interest in the Editor's curiosity, the entertainment provided *him* by the Publisher's monomania, the reader's amused disdain for the strange ineffectuality which accompanies the Narrator's boldness of plan, the dawning recognition that the Scoundrel's "intercourse with the Misses Bordereau," and the consequent spectacle, have not yet proved to be the intimacy and drama that his plan leads one to expect.

Aspern's collaboration is of longer duration and more intimate, for in the Publisher's haunted recollection his deeds summon up (by a roundabout implication, to be sure) the poet whose papers he seeks to possess and publish, and whose relation with Juliana Bordereau was at once the redeeming intimacy and the betrayal which the Editor's affair with Juliana and Miss Tina ludicrously, grotesquely reenacts. The Scoundrel's tendency to associate himself with his idol is the measure not only of his vanity but of real connections which exert their pressure on the story's diction. The "critic" and "historian" is nonetheless " 'a poor devil of a man of letters,' " who has "always some business of writing in hand." By the time Miss Tina finally asks him " 'Do you write—do you write?' " and " 'Do you write about *him*—do you pry into his life?' " the ironic analogy between the Publishing Scoundrel's affair and the writer's is clearly projected in the weird hallucinations which are the product of the Editor's original scheme and his haunted recapitulation of it. The Editor remarks early that Aspern "had been kinder and more considerate than in his place—if I could imagine myself in any such box—I should have found the trick of," and the "combination of arts" which he eventually employs to negotiate with the Bordereaus places himself in precisely that box by the time he invades Juliana's apartment and rifles her desk. The analogy is deepened later when he confronts the prospect of marriage with Miss Tina and brushes against a plan for an alternative which crosses his mind ("I mightn't unite myself, yet I might still have what she had") without bringing him to identify the alternative as either theft or an illicit affair.

The ironic association between the publishing Editor (on his "eccentric private errand") and the publishing poet on the errand of art, which is completed later in the story, is anticipated in the imaginary conversations which the Scoundrel constructs with the poet whom he calls his "prompter" in the drama. "Invoked" and hovering, Aspern's ghost accompanies the Scoundrel as if "he regarded the affair as his own no less than as mine" and assures him that Juliana " 'was very attractive in 1820. Meanwhile, aren't we in Venice together, and what better place is there for the meeting of dear friends?' " When Tina first displays signs of love, Aspern's painted portrait seems "to smile . . . with mild mockery; he might have been amused at my case," and when her touching, desperate invitation to marriage is tendered, the portrait, with an "odd expression" on its face, seems to taunt: " 'Get out of it as you can, my dear fellow!' "

This is the voice of the poet who had met Juliana (so the Editor concludes) on the errand of art while sitting for a portrait in her father's studio, and who had had the boldness and passion to enter into an affair with her in the 1820s, but who (so the impression was in 1825) "had 'treated her badly' " and left her with the deeply ingrained suspicions which Miss Tina thinks stem from " 'something—ages before I was born—in [Juliana's] life,' " namely the love affair to which the papers are thought to allude. Although Aspern's published poems are less ambiguous than Shakespeare's sonnets, it is difficult "to put one's finger on the passage in which [Juliana's] fair fame suffered injury"; yet it is pertinent to ask if the rumors about Juliana's "impenitent passion" and tarnished respectability are substantiated by the poetry of the American who wrote when "our native land was nude and crude" and who in that enviable freedom was able "to feel, understand and express everything." Were the rumors "a sign that the singer had *betrayed* her, had *given her away*, as we say nowadays, to posterity?" The phrases (which I have italicized) transform each other into puns, and suggest that Aspern both commemorated his beloved and exposed his mistress, that he both immortalized and victimized his Juliana in betraying or giving her away to posterity.

These rumors, hypotheses, and queries are all parts of the Editor's mere theories about Aspern's life and Juliana's past conduct (he had "hatched a little romance" about her expatriation), and along with his constructed conversations with Aspern are part of his twisted recollection. Yet in them emerges an authentic picture, though a fantastic image rather than a strictly accurate portrait, of Jeffrey Aspern. The painted miniature portrait, executed by Juliana's father, which the Editor accepts as a gift from Miss Tina and then pays a huge price for, is at once a Rorschach blot for the exercise of the Historian's imagination and a speaking image of the strange Orpheus who loved Juliana and used her to the profit of art.

Orpheus as a prototype for Aspern occurs to the Scoundrel early in the tale when thinking of the throngs of women who had "flung themselves at his head" and when excusing the injuries that were bound to occur "while the fury raged"; the Editor exclaims: " 'Orpheus and the Maenads!' " The shade of Orpheus emerges again momentarily when the Editor speaks of Aspern hanging, like Orpheus's lyre, "high in the heaven of our literature" and when he raises the question of Aspern's loyalty to Juliana. The Editor mentions Aspern's return to Europe and his claim in one poem "that he had come back for her sake"; the Editor hopes that the voyage was for her sake and not "just for the phrase."

While in these instances the figure of Orpheus, seeking to be reunited with his love, is ironically associated with Aspern specifically, it functions more allusively and pervasively in the tale because so circumscribed an identification is impossible under the pressure of the story's action and form. The introduction of Orpheus proves to be apt for the very reason that it seems, on first encounter but also subsequently, to be oddly far-fetched. Introduced in the third paragraph, the legendary associations are in keeping with the contortions, the multiple refractions of association, the proliferation of displacements and substitutions, which characterize the Gothic form; they serve to precipitate out the ambiguities of the Orpheus legend and scatter its implications in stark and twisted versions. The result is that the legend of Orpheus, the Maenads, and Eurydice does not so much separate opposing sides in a tragic struggle as shape an action in which characters are mutually engaged, define the process of their interaction, and suggest the contingent possibilities, frenzied and controlled, destructive and creative, of their interaction. The legend's relevance is all the more weird for the fact that the Historian's information is and must be rife with conjecture, hearsay, and evidential inference, including the "very strong presumption" (but little more) that any papers exist at all. The tale hovers, to its peril but with its corresponding boldness, on the brink of utter historical uncertainty which is ludicrous and terrifying. And in the negotiations among Aspern, Juliana, Tina, and the Scoundrel the ghost of Orpheus —so passionate for his Eurydice yet so distant from her and from all other women afterward—is crossed with the masculine femininity of George Sand, the devotee of passion who outlived but used and celebrated it, a pale victim nonetheless triumphant against the siege of all the years.

If the divine Aspern was the supreme lyricist and may have made a second trip across the waters for Juliana's sake, he is seen now in the company of a male friend, having replaced the Editor's collaborator Cumnor as a companion; his voice is present now in a " 'dying fall.' "

Yet this Orpheus never married, and Juliana is an oddly unspliced Eurydice. And if she is passionate in devotion to the memory of their love, pitiable in her tomb-like isolation from the present, and pathetic in her attempt to honor the relics of their love by keeping them in a trunk and planning to burn them finally rather than to violate their privacy, there is also an uncanny strength and a weird craft in the feat which the battered woman performs on her deathbed to balk the predatory maneuvers of the Editor, whom she has discovered rummaging her desk: single-handed she removes the papers from the trunk, thrusts them into her bed, and sews them up between the mattresses. Her motive is to secure the papers, but her logic is an extension of the Scoundrel's, who suspected that she had "consigned her relics to her bedroom," perhaps to "some battered box that was shoved under the bed, to the drawer of some lame dressing-table" or to her desk, a "receptacle somewhat infirm but still capable of keeping rare secrets." The infirm woman's act is in strange keeping not only with her now desperate attempt to protect the integrity of her love but with the strategy she has been pursuing since renting rooms to the Scoundrel, the scheme of using the papers and the affair they image to entice from him the favor of money.

The Editor early found it unnerving that "these women so associated with Aspern should so constantly bring the pecuniary question back," and whether Juliana is teasing him with allusions to her "rapture" or keeping Aspern "buried in her soul," the signs of her "acquisitive propensity" loom large in the Editor's recollection. When he agrees to pay, three months in advance, the huge rent she has long managed to live without, Juliana exclaims "almost gaily: 'He'll give three thousand—three thousand tomorrow!'" It is she who thinks the Historian should sell the surplus bloom of the garden he has grown to beguile his hostesses and who proposes to sell the portrait of Aspern for a staggering thousand pounds. Indeed, with her (as with George Sand) the "vision of pecuniary profit was most what drew out the divine Juliana." Behind the green eye-shade which screens her actual attitude from the Scoundrel, the old woman is "full of craft." (James had been told that "George Sand looked a great deal on the ground . . . that one felt shut off from her by a sort of veil or film.") And while her conversation (like the Scoundrel's narrative) permits glimpses of the bliss she recalls, it yields occasionally also the "old-time tone" or "caper" of the shrewd bargainer which the Editor's idolization has obscured, the incipient shrewdness that has become more pronounced and justified since Aspern left her and since the well-heeled Scoundrel, presenting the occasion for profit, has appeared at her door as a possible "victim" and virtually "taught her to calculate."

What the Editor comes to see gradually is that Juliana seeks money for Tina's sake, and that her maneuvering behind her green shade in her combat with him is as cagily strategic as his siege, and that it is founded, like his tactics, on the "fruitful idea" of gaining acquaintance through intimacy. Coaching Miss Tina and luring on the Editor, the "supersensuous grandmother" who has "outlived passions and faculties" nevertheless shows signs of her "adventurous youth"; she is not only engaged in combat that is partly defensive and partly vindictive but is nursing along an affair, as her fears and hopes are transferred to the plight of her niece. Miss Tina, middle-aged but "amiable and unencumbered," is a "parti"; and Juliana, disdainful though she is of her ward's shyness and her lodger's bower of bloom, seeks to secure happiness for Tina in love. Her last encounter with the Editor is the one that renders her speechless and precipitates her death, but she manages on her deathbed, through "'signs'" as Tina explains later, to suggest to Tina the import and pressure of Juliana's desire: despite the fact that she should burn the papers, Tina clearly favors the Historian and his idea of publishing them, and consequently Juliana would consent, for the sake of her niece, if the Scoundrel were to become "'a relation.'" Whether or not the "relation" Juliana had in mind were necessarily marriage (the marriage she had done without but may have learned to hope and bargain for), marriage becomes the aim of Tina; and while the Editor stands "pensively, awkwardly, grotesquely" declaring "'It wouldn't do, it wouldn't do!'" he recognizes that in the affair he has undertaken, marriage has come to be "the price."

It is the Historian, first and foremost, who has undertaken the Orphic task of retrieving the papers from their tomb and resurrecting the dead in reawakening Juliana and quickening Tina to an interest in life. And it is he, though he is without "the tradition of personal conquest" and must now protest his manliness, who gets caught in the dream of marriage which had been Orpheus' bond of love. The courtship of Tina was, to begin with, the unscrupulous expedient which the Editor proposed half-jokingly to Mrs. Prest as the means he might employ to get the papers. But it has been transformed into the desperate commitment which he faces as the dream of marriage comes to life across the chasm of the years to become the pathetic hope of Tina's waning future. Marriage becomes the instrument by which the Editor may not only redeem his campaign to capture the papers but make good on the antic courtship which his scheme, Mrs. Prest's fruitful idea, and his courtly conduct have turned into.

In the course of his affair he is haunted by examples of other heroes— lovers and warriors whose careers are echoed in his imagination and in the painting and statuary he consults for advice, and whose success exacerbates his self-consciousness. The painted ghost of Orpheus beams encouragingly, then taunts his strangely unmaniacal devotee. The Editor's servant Pasquale enjoys the frequent visits of a "young lady with a powdered face" and is friendly also with the household maids, and during a visit with one of them to Juliana's sick chamber "Pasquale peep[s] over the doctor's shoulder" while the physician eyes the Editor, an odd Musset, as if "taking me for a rival who had the field before him." The equestrian statue of Marcus Aurelius, benign and bestride, is far away in Rome, the Editor recalls, but in Venice one of "the finest of all mounted figures," a statue of the *condottiere* Colleoni, stares indifferently past the hesitant Historian, engrossed probably in "battles and strategems" of "a different quality from any I had to tell him of." Yet the preoccupations of that mercenary mounted warrior—like those of the Maenads and George Sand, Orpheus and de Musset—do define the complex irony of the Narrator's courtship-siege, which penetrates far into the buried past and chambered present he seeks to enter but winds up finally balked, in actual deed and in the Historian's compulsive reconstruction of it.

As in the displacements of a fantastic dream, the Historian's anticipated expenses, lavish but vaguely budgeted, recede behind Juliana's demand for a huge rent; the papers (first hidden in a trunk) are shifted to the mattresses of Juliana's deathbed, to reappear, locked up by Tina, in the desk where the Scoundrel had first rummaged for them, then disappear in flames; the coveted papers, the relics of love, are displaced by the "careful," "elegant" portrait; and Aspern's presence, presumably mediated by his poetry, is mediated also by the green shade and wily craft of Juliana, to be echoed finally, in a dying fall, in Tina's and the Scoundrel's awakening to the dream and the entanglements of love.

Both that awakening and its betrayal are entailed in the courtship-siege which takes form as the Historian's plans are translated into performance, as his actions and motives are recapitulated in memory, and as the stunned recognition which his deeds and recollections yield is presented in the fantastic account which he constructs and renders with such finesse. The vocabularies of war and love and commerce are joined in a grotesquely ironic suspension. The boldness of the delineations, and the contrasts of character and motive, which are intensified under pressures which force them into closer contact and even fuse them, mark the narrative as a parody —in visual terms, a caricature. When the Narrator undertakes to " 'work the garden' " and recalls that "I would batter the old women with lilies—I would bombard their citadel with roses. Their door would have to yield to the pressure when a mound of fragrance should be heaped against it"—his outlandish declarations project at once the love affair which his conduct simulates and increasingly approximates, the campaign he wages as he invades Juliana's room and desk, and the acquisitive enterprise which resembles increasingly the burglary he denies intending when he presses the button of Juliana's secretary, intending "not to do anything, not even . . . to let down the lid" but solely "to test my theory, to see if the cover *would* move." The images, with the actions and motives they express, take the measure of each other, suggesting at once the Editor's cross-purposes, the extent of his success, and his final ineffectuality. His engaging tactics bring him closer to, but fail to culminate in, the marriage Tina longs for; his courtly siege reaches the fortress but terminates in embarrassed retreat; his expensive suit brings him closer to the papers he would gladly buy but results in their permanent removal from the market.

His is a compound recognition of his ineffectuality as warrior, lover, and bargaining historian, and of his guilt for the deeds he *has* perpetrated. His recollections avoid the easy dichotomies of credit and condemnation, and the blatant antitheses of radiant innocence and utter depravity, but the tale is founded on an intimate confession which is the more effective and vivid because it takes account of the complexities of the experience which the Narrator and the others undergo. Accordingly the tale is permeated by the "moral sense" and moral courage which James dwelt on in *Partial Portraits* and located close to the "artistic sense" in the artist's mind. From the earliest paragraphs of the story on, for all the Editor's bland decorum, the feelings of guilt are apparent even when showing faintly beneath broader strokes of reckless, unscrupulous editorial enterprise. In the course of the narrative these feelings become pronounced and more nakedly revealed until, in crucial moments, they match in vivid intensity the grotesquely evil intentions he displays. His violations of Juliana's privacy and Tina's trust become increasingly outrageous, yet he becomes more candidly conscience stricken about them, welcoming the opportunity to divulge his aim and his identity to Tina while enlisting her as a cohort.

If the bald contrast of these conflicting emotions reveals the form of caricature, the effect is enforced by pressures bearing on the action for which the Narrator is not alone accountable, though his recognitions and re-enactment bring them into the narrative which he constructs. The figure of Aspern rises from the past to haunt the narrative: a model of love, profitable conquest, and expressive power which images both the consummations of love and art and their betrayals which the Scoundrel's efforts render in debased and antic form. Juliana emerges from her tomb-like isolation, affording the prospect of entertainment to Mrs. Prest and profitable success to the Historian, and risks the gambits of love and commerce for Tina, with all the craft of an artist and the bargaining power of an extortionist. Tina emerges from seclusion, pathetically but ludicrously helpless in her innocence, coached and thrust before the Historian by her shrewd aunt, liberated by the Historian's intrusion in her life which culminates when (at Juliana's cruelly blunt insistence) he takes Tina to St. Mark's Square; her "return to society" is marked by her "theorising about prices" of merchandise, her "spirits" are "revived" by "the sight of the bright shop-windows." It is she finally who acts on the proposition that the Editor might gain acquaintance with the papers through the intimacy of marriage and bargains to that end in her next-to-last interview with the Scoundrel. The motives which impel the Historian are not peculiar to him, and accordingly the contortions of caricature are features of the story's action as well as of its portraits. The fantastic delineations, the bold strokes, mark the lines which divide but also visually join the area of willed action to the realm of inescapable conditions which impinge on the effort to " 'rake up' " and resurrect the past, " 'violating a tomb' " to penetrate and take possession whether in the art of entertainment or the commerce of love. The fantastic proliferation of lovers, the mounting payments of rent, the multiplying series of mediators between the Editor's present and the past, between him and the love, possession, and expressive power which are imaged in the coveted papers—these respond to pressures which pervade and lie deep within the story and press its incidents into a drama founded on caricature.

The combination of the ludicrous and the horrible are piercingly comic in one crucial incident which joins the gestures of love and utilitarian transactions to those of the historical imagination. The Editor hopes to reach Aspern's past by shaking Juliana's hand, sealing their verbal contract for rent. But when his "desire to hold in my own for a moment the hand Jeffrey Aspern had pressed" is balked by Juliana's refusal, he turns to Tina instead, exclaiming " 'Oh you'll do as well' " and Juliana demands coolly: " 'Shall you bring the money in gold?' " Compressed into the incident is the very crux of the drama, the transference of the Historian's effort from Juliana to Tina and the ironic analogy between his expedient affair and that of Aspern.

The caricature is less relaxed, more cruel in the scene where the Scoundrel, pressing the button of Juliana's desk, turns to find that the aged woman is watching him. The "pale forewarned victim" and the Editor with the "historic sense" are at last "face to face." The confrontation is unrelieved, and the Narrator's confession is stark in its candor, as he recalls that Juliana, in her nightdress with her hands raised in condemnation, "had lifted the everlasting curtain that covered half her face" and that "for the first, the last, the only time" he "beheld her extraordinary eyes." Her glaring eyes "were like the sudden drench, for a caught burglar, of a flood of gaslight; they made me horribly ashamed." Memory is no safe refuge from the pathos and dignity of her emaciated figure: "I never shall forget her strange little bent white tottering figure, with its lifted head, her attitude, her expression." Nor is his stammered excuse that he "meant no harm" a protection from the force with which she "hissed out passionately, furiously: 'Ah you publishing scoundrel' " and fell back "with a quick spasm, as if death had descended on her, into Miss Tina's arms."

The mode of caricature has become the instrument of tragedy by the time Tina, who prevented Juliana from burning the papers before she died, tries to redeem her effort and the gambits of both Juliana and the Editor in her last interviews with the Historian. Her "cry of desolation" when faced with separation from the Editor, the sobbing which resounds "in the great empty hall" after she has offered " 'everything' " to him, are tragically genuine. Yet her awkwardness, though touching, is pronounced, and the aim of her efforts is clearly calculated. When she suggests that if he were a "relation" he might see the papers, she talks in quickening phrases with a compressed subtlety of implications which combine heartfelt intensity with the sureness of a desperately rehearsed performance, "as if speaking words got by heart." She pursues her pathetic aim with "transparent astuteness" and after giving the painted portrait of Aspern to the Historian as a present and proposing " 'Couldn't we sell it?' " her proposal that they join in the commercial traffic is a ludicrous but touching parody of the dream of marriage she clings to: " 'We can divide the money.' "

The Historian's precipitous flight from "the poor deluded infatuated extravagant lady" is an embarrassed, nerveless retreat, an abdication of his mission; he seeks refuge in an opportunism sanctioned by Aspern's example (" 'Get out of it as you can, my dear fellow!' ") and in the comfort of moralism ("my predicament was the just punishment of that most fatal of . . . follies, our not having known when to stop"), but neither the equestrian statues which haunt him nor the importunities of his own mind during sleep will let him rest in the certainty that "I couldn't, for a bundle of tattered papers, marry a ridiculous pathetic provincial old woman." The very atmosphere of Venice prepares for the transformation into drama which the closing pages accomplish. Piazza San Marco now resembles simultaneously a domestic residence (a "splendid common domicile, familiar domestic and resonant") and a "theatre with its actors clicking over bridges," a "stage" with the Venetians becoming the "members of an endless dramatic troupe." The drama hinges finally on two events which take place in the same house on the same night: Tina's secret burning of the papers and the sudden resurgence of the Editor's determination to acquire them.

The Scoundrel recalls jumping from bed in the morning, instantly aware that during the night his determination to see Tina again had revived, and feeling like one who has "left the house-door ajar or a candle burning," wondering "Was I still in time to save my goods?" His "passionate appreciation of Juliana's treasure" has returned, and he begins to ponder some way of gaining possession of the papers without marrying Tina. He is still trying to invent or name an alternative when Tina admits him to Juliana's "forlorn parlour" for their final interview.

The Miss Tina whom he confronts has undergone a "rare alteration" which the Editor's preoccupation with "strategems and spoils" had prevented his anticipating, although ironically his machinations, and his failure to press them to completion, have helped produce the transformation. Unknown to him and to the reader, she has burned the papers, we learn later, consumed by the "sense of her failure" to win the Editor's love and consent to marriage and convinced that she has no reason now to keep them. What is significant about the form of the story at this point is that three events, on three different occasions, are made to coalesce by the story's form: the burning of the papers, the Historian's and Tina's separation the next day, and the Historian's recapitulation (some weeks or months later) of the incidents in memory and in his account. The act of burning the papers is made inseparable from the Editor's reconstruction of his discovery of their loss, and both the destruction of the papers and the Editor's account are rendered through the drama of Tina's transfiguring performance in the closing interview. The sacrifice which she performed and suffered when she burned the papers and the drama later of her separation from the Historian, are inextricably fused; the story is so constructed that together these occasions become the sacrificial foundation of the Scoundrel's narrative enactment. As a consequence, the burning of the papers is made an image of the betrayals and wastage which recur in the story—but also an image of the intense passion which produced the "shreds and relics" of Aspern's affair with Juliana, and produced the dream of love which is consecrated by Tina's pathetic sacrifice and commemorated by the Historian.

Tina has done not simply the *right thing* (too long delayed) nor the *wrong thing* but, as she puts it, the " 'great thing' ": the only gesture — ruinously, regrettably destructive, intensely expressive, faithful to the passion the papers symbolize, and certain to be gripping in its impact on the Historian—the only act which is now adequate to the tragic experience which has ensued. The burden of Tina's final interview with the Editor— she might have refused to see him, and left him in the dark—is to redeem her act in the drama of their separation. That she does so is owing to the new "force of soul" created in her by the experience she has undergone and to the firmness of her sustained performance. She becomes, with "every paper burnt," the "pale forewarned victim," triumphant in the "tower of art" and the "citadel of style." And it is her last look back at the Editor, and her acceptance of his money for the painted portrait of Aspern, that frustrate and complete, distort and express, betray and reveal the denouement of Orpheus' mission.

She "had strung herself up to accepting" their separation, and the "rare alteration" in her spirit enables her "in her abjection" to "smile strangely, with an infinite gentleness" at the Scoundrel. The "look of forgiveness, of absolution" which she gives him is the "magic" of her spirit, the effective "trick" of "her expression." The effect is to transfigure Tina—"she was younger, she was not a ridiculous old woman"—and simultaneously to bring the Scoundrel farther than he has yet come on the voyage of love—to the brink of marriage and (he thinks) success: "I heard a whisper somewhere in the depths of my conscience: 'Why not, after all—why not?' It seemed to me I *could* pay the price." Yet the whisper is supplanted by the stronger note of Tina's voice, sounding her farewell with wishes for his happiness; she is acting out the separation she had "strung herself up to accepting," the tragic anticipation which had transfigured her and stirred the Editor's will and conscience.

Her smile is part of a deliberately controlled performance. With her "gentleness" she tells him nonetheless firmly that "'I shall not see you again. I don't want to'" and finally divulges the information in a piercingly effective sequence that she had not only destroyed the papers but that she did so "'one by one, in the kitchen,'" and that the process "'took a long time'" because "'there were so many.'" In the harsh glare of this exposure of his baseness and futility, the Editor recognizes that Tina's transfiguration is over and that she is again a "plain dingy elderly person." Her last remark is both an expression of moral revulsion and a recognition of tragic necessity: "'I can't stay with you longer, I can't.'" In a strangely twisted version of Orpheus' separation from Eurydice, *she* turns her back on *him*, but then pauses to look back once, giving him the "one look" that marks their separation but grips his memory: "I have never forgotten it and I sometimes still suffer from it, though it was not resentful." The Scoundrel's last effort is to pay for the portrait of Aspern which Tina gave him, a substitute for the papers and his hopes but an image of them which he possesses and keeps above his desk. Pretending to sell the painting, he sends Tina a sum much larger than its market value in an effort to compensate for his deeds and to express his gratitude. Her last gesture is to keep the money, "with thanks."

These transactions parody the experience they supplant, yet like the painted portrait of Aspern, they recall the exploits and the sacrificial drama which brought the portrait to light, recall *all* that is implicit in the Historian's closing declaration: "I can scarcely bear my loss—I mean of the precious papers." Thanks to the sacrificial drama which Tina's action constitutes, the painted portrait is resurrected and acquired, the transactions are completed, and the entertaining narrative is constructed and presented, but these are accomplished at the expense of a more complete vision, a more intimate communion, and a more appropriate form, which the story's brilliant art can create as possibilities only in the torment of betraying them.

"Daisy Miller": A Study of Changing Intentions

Carol Ohmann

Henry James's most popular nouvelle seems to have owed its initial promi-
nence as much to the controversy it provoked as to the artistry it displayed.
"Daisy Miller" caused a bitter dispute in the customarily urbane dining
room of Mrs. Lynn Linton; it gave American writers of etiquette a satis-
fying opportunity to chastise native mothers and daughters (Daisy should
have had a chaperone; dear reader, take heed); it brought Henry James
himself, while he sat in the confines of a Venetian gondola, a round scolding
from a highly articulate woman of the cosmopolitan world. The causes of
argument, of course, were the character of James's heroine and the judgment her creator made of her. In late Victorian eyes, Daisy was likely to be
either wholly innocent or guilty; James, either all for her or against her.

Today, Daisy's notoriety attends her only in her fictional world. We
take her now as one of our familiars; we invoke her, in the assurance that
she will come and be recognized, as an American figure both vital and
prototypical. Thus Ihab Hassan, for example, joins her in his *Radical Innocence* with Twain's Huck Finn and Crane's Henry Fleming, and notes that
all three are young protagonists faced with "the first existential ordeal,
crisis, or encounter with experience." Taking Daisy with appreciation and
without alarm, we also re-read her character and re-evaluate her moral
status. We seem to meet James's sophistication with our own, by agreeing
on a mixed interpretation of Daisy: she is literally innocent, but she is also
ignorant and incautious. Or, as F. W. Dupee writes, and his view meets
with considerable agreement elsewhere in our criticism, "[Daisy] does

From *American Literature* 36, no. 1 (March 1964). © 1964 by Duke University Press.

what she likes because she hardly knows what else to do. Her will is at once strong and weak by reason of the very indistinctness of her general aims."

Our near consensus of opinion on "Daisy Miller" seems to me largely correct. I certainly do not want to dismiss it, although I do wish to elaborate upon it and ground it in Jamesian text and method. At the same time, however, I wish to suggest that our very judiciousness is supported by only part of James's nouvelle and that other parts, certain scenes in Rome, really call for franker and more intense alignments of both sympathy and judgment. In a sense, the early and extreme reactions to Daisy were adequate responses to James's creation. Whether black or white, these responses did at least perceive that the final issue of the nouvelle was a matter of total commitment. In short, I think James began writing with one attitude toward his heroine and concluded with a second and different attitude toward her.

I

James begins his nouvelle by building a dramatic, and largely comic, contrast between two ways of responding to experience—a contrast at once suggested by the first-person narrator in the opening paragraph:

> in the month of June, American travellers are extremely numerous; it may be said, indeed, that Vevey assumes at this period some of the characteristics of an American watering-place. There are sights and sounds which evoke a vision, an echo, of Newport and Saratoga. There is a flitting hither and thither of "stylish" young girls, a rustling of muslin flounces, a rattle of dance-music in the morning hours, a sound of high-pitched voices at all times. You receive an impression of these things at the excellent inn of the "Trois Couronnes," and are transported in fancy to the Ocean House or to Congress Hall. But at the "Trois Couronnes," it must be added, there are other features that are much at variance with these suggestions: neat German waiters, who look like secretaries of legation; Russian princesses sitting in the garden; little Polish boys walking about, held by the hand, with their governors.

The carefree exuberance, the noisy frivolity, of the American visitors is set against the quiet formality and restraint of the Europeans, who hold even their little boys in check.

James repeats his opening contrast in virtually every piece of dialogue that follows. While the hero Frederick Winterbourne is an American by birth, he has lived "a long time" in Geneva, the "little metropolis of Calvinism," the "dark old city at the other end of the lake." And Winterbourne's mode of speech suggests the extent to which he has become Europeanized. In Vevey, he finds himself "at liberty," on a little holiday from Geneva. He takes a daring plunge into experience; with no more than a very casual introduction from her little brother Randolph, he speaks to Daisy Miller. "This little boy and I have made acquaintance," he says. Daisy glances at him and turns away. In a moment, Winterbourne tries again. "Are you going to Italy?" he asks. Daisy says, "Yes, sir," and no more. "Are you—a—going over the Simplon?" Winterbourne continues. Shortly afterwards, as Daisy continues to ignore him, Winterbourne "risk[s] an observation upon the beauty of the view." Winterbourne's feelings of "liberty" and of "risk" and, later, of "audacity" become ironic in conjunction with his speech. For all his holiday spirit, his language is studiously formal, his opening conversational bits, unimaginative and conventional.

In opposition to Winterbourne, Daisy often speaks in the language of extravagant, if unoriginal, enthusiasm. In her opinion, Europe is "perfectly sweet. . . . She had ever so many intimate friends that had been there ever so many times. . . . she had had ever so many dresses and things from Paris." She wants to go to the Castle of Chillon "dreadfully." Or, unlike Winterbourne again, Daisy speaks in an idiom that is homely and matter-of-fact. When Winterbourne asks, "Your brother is not interested in ancient monuments?" she rejects his formal phrasing and says simply, "[Randolph] says he don't care much about old castles."

For all their differences, Winterbourne and Daisy may still be capable of *rapprochement*. Toward the end of part 1, Daisy teases Winterbourne out of his formality and makes him, for a moment, speak her language — makes him, for a moment, express himself enthusiastically. "Do, then, let me give you a row," Winterbourne says. Daisy replies, "It's quite lovely, the way you say that!" And Winterbourne answers, "It will be still more lovely to do it." Winterbourne is, and Daisy notices this, a "mixture." He is not quite, or at least not yet, thoroughly Europeanized.

Winterbourne may be influenced by Daisy, but he is also subject to the sway of his aunt. Mrs. Costello is a woman of few words. When Winterbourne asks her, in Vevey, if she has observed Mrs. Miller, Daisy, and Randolph, she raps out the reply: "Oh, yes, I have observed them. Seen them—heard them—and kept out of their way." Epigram is Mrs. Costello's favorite way of speaking and perfectly expresses the inflexibility of her approach to experience. Her principles of value have long been set—she need only apply them. Whatever is vulgar, whatever is improper, she condemns out of hand, and shuns. Sage and spokesman of the American set abroad, she guards a *style* of life and reveals its furthest limit of permissible emotion by exclaiming, "I am an old woman, but I am not too old—thank Heaven—to be shocked!"

The opening, then, and indeed the chief focus of "Daisy Miller" is a comic portrayal of different ways of living, different manners. In the social settings with which they are identified, in the ways they speak, as well as in what they say, the various characters range themselves along an axis that runs from the natural to the cultivated, from the exuberant to the restrained.

In the conflict between Geneva and Schenectady, there is, I think, little doubt of the direction James gives our sympathies. Presented with the collision between the artificial and the natural, the restrained and the free, we side emotionally with Daisy. We sympathize with Winterbourne, too, to the extent that he seems capable of coming "alive" and to the extent that he speaks up in favor of Daisy to Mrs. Costello in Vevey and, later, in Rome, to Mrs. Costello and also to Mrs. Walker, another American who has lived in Geneva. For the rest, however, our emotional alliance with Winterbourne is disturbed or interrupted by his Genevan penchant for criticism. At his first meeting with Daisy in Vevey, Winterbourne mentally accuses her—"very forgivingly—of a want of finish." But when Daisy blithely announces that she has always had "a great deal of gentlemen's society," Winterbourne is more alarmed. He wonders if he must accuse her of "actual or potential *inconduite*, as they said at Geneva."

In Rome, although Winterbourne defends Daisy to the American colony publicly, he is, privately, increasingly shocked by her friendship with the "third-rate" Italian Giovanelli. Her walks with Giovanelli, her rides with Giovanelli, her tête-à-têtes in her own drawing room with Giovanelli—all worry Winterbourne. He imitates Mrs. Walker in scolding Daisy. And so he removes himself farther and farther from her. When he finally comes upon her with Giovanelli in the Colosseum at night, he thinks that she has certainly compromised herself. And he is relieved. For his personal feelings for Daisy have gradually been overwhelmed by his intellectual involvement in the problem of Daisy. He is relieved and "exhilarated" that the "riddle" has suddenly become "easy to read." He promptly judges Daisy by her manners—as Mrs. Costello and Mrs. Walker have already done—and condemns her. "What a clever little reprobate she was," he thinks, "and how smartly she played at injured innocence!"

He learns otherwise too late. He knows, for a moment at the end of the nouvelle, that he has made a mistake; he knows he has wronged Daisy because he has stayed too long abroad, has become too rigid in his values. Yet his knowledge does not change him. The authorial voice concludes the tale by mocking Winterbourne's return to the narrow social code of restraint and prejudice:

> Nevertheless, he went back to live at Geneva, whence there continue to come the most contradictory accounts of his motives of sojourn: a report that he is "studying" hard—an intimation that he is much interested in a very clever foreign lady.

Like so many Jamesian heroes, Winterbourne has lost the capacity for love, and he has lost the opportunity to come to life.

As Winterbourne judges Daisy, judges her unfairly, and completes her expulsion from the American set in Rome, our sympathy for her naturally increases. But I think James does not—save through a certain pattern of symbolic imagery to which I wish to return in a moment—guide us to any such simple intellectual alignment with his American heroine.

Daisy's sensibility has very obvious limitations, limitations we hear very clearly in the statement that Europe is "perfectly sweet." Daisy is more intensely alive than anyone else we meet in Vevey or Rome. But James hints from time to time at a possible richness of aesthetic experience that is beyond Daisy's capabilities—a richness that would include an appreciation of the artificial, or the cultivated, not as it is represented by the mores of Geneva but by the "splendid chants and organ-tones" of St. Peter's and by the "superb portrait of Innocent X. by Velasquez."

And Daisy has other limitations. The members of the American community abroad are very much aware of one another's existence. True, they use their mutual awareness to no good purpose—they are watchbirds watching one another for vulgarity, for any possible lapse from propriety. But Daisy's social awareness is so primitive as scarcely to exist. At Rome, in the Colosseum, Winterbourne's imagination cannot stretch to include the notion of unsophisticated innocence. But neither can Daisy's imagination stretch to include the idea that manners really matter to those who practice them. She never realizes the consternation she causes in Rome. "I don't believe it," she says to Winterbourne. "They are only pretending to be shocked." Her blindness to the nature of the American colony is equalled by her blindness to Winterbourne and Giovanelli as individuals. While Winterbourne fails to "read" her "riddle" rightly, she fails to "read" his. She feels his disapproval in Rome, but she is not aware of his affection for her. Neither does she reveal any adequate perception of her impact on Giovanelli. To Daisy, going about with Mr. Giovanelli is very good fun. Giovanelli's feelings, we learn at the end, have been much more seriously involved.

James therefore hands a really favorable intellectual judgment to neither Geneva nor Schenectady. He gives his full approval neither to the manners of restraint nor to those of freedom. His irony touches Daisy as well as the Europeanized Americans. And the accumulation of his specific ironies hints at an ideal of freedom and of vitality and also of æsthetic and social awareness that is nowhere fully exemplified in the nouvelle. To be from Schenectady, to be from the new world, is to be free from the restrictions of Geneva. But merely to be free is not enough.

II

Such, then, in some detail are the Jamesian dynamics of social contrast that give us our prudent estimate of Daisy—a heroine innocent and exuberant and free, but also unreflective and insensible of the world around her. But, as I have already suggested, this estimate does not receive support from the whole of the story. To begin with, prudence leads straight to the conclusion that Daisy dies as a result of social indiscretion. What began as a comedy of manners, ends in the pathos, if not the tragedy, of a lonely Roman deathbed and burial. And there is, it seems to me, in this progress from the Trois Couronnes to the Protestant cemetery a change in tone so pronounced, a breach in cause and appropriate effect so wide, as to amount to a puzzling disruption of James's artistry.

To be sure, James tries to make Daisy's death inevitable, and to make it so within, as it were, the boundaries of his comedy of manners. Early in part 2, at Mrs. Walker's late one afternoon, Daisy remarks that she is going to take a walk on the Pincian Hill with Giovanelli. Mrs. Walker tries to dissuade her from the impropriety—a walk at such a time in such a place with such a dubious companion. It isn't "safe," Mrs. Walker says, while Mrs. Miller adds, "You'll get the fever as sure as you live." And Daisy herself, as she walks towards the Pincian Hill with Winterbourne, alludes to the fever: "We are going to stay [in Rome] all winter—if we don't die of the fever; and I guess we'll stay then."

With these remarks, James foreshadows Daisy's death, and links her fate with her carelessness of the manners of restraint. But these preparations do not successfully solve his difficulties either of tone or of cause and effect.

They croak disaster far too loudly, far too obviously, and, still, the punishment no more fits the crime than it does in a typical cautionary tale.

In part 1, James has already used the words "natural," "uncultivated," and "fresh" to describe his heroine. And in the choice of the name, Daisy, he may have suggested her simplicity and her spontaneous beauty. In part 2, just after the opening scene at Mrs. Walker's, James follows up the implications of these epithets—"natural," "uncultivated," "fresh"—and of the name Daisy and gives them a somewhat different significance.

In Rome, after Winterbourne has been taken up in Mrs. Walker's carriage and set down again, he sees Daisy with Giovanelli in a natural setting—a setting that James describes in brilliant and expansive terms. Daisy and Giovanelli are in the Pincian Garden overlooking the Villa Borghese:

> They evidently saw no one; they were too deeply occupied with each other. When they reached the low garden-wall they stood a moment looking off at the great flat-topped pine-clusters of the Villa Borghese; then Giovanelli seated himself, familiarly, upon the broad ledge of the wall. The western sun in the opposite sky sent out a brilliant shaft through a couple of cloud-bars, whereupon Daisy's companion took her parasol out of her hands and opened it. She came a little nearer and he held the parasol over her; then, still holding it, he let it rest upon her shoulder, so that both of their heads were hidden from Winterbourne. This young man lingered a moment, then he began to walk. But he walked—not towards the couple with the parasol; towards the residence of his aunt, Mrs. Costello.

This scene links Daisy with the natural world, and links her with that world more closely than any other scene James has so far given us. And it suggests that the distance between Winterbourne and Daisy is greater even than the distance that separates artificial from natural manners, greater than the distance that separates restraint from free self-expression.

That suggestion becomes a certainty on the Palatine Hill:

> A few days after his brief interview with her mother, [Winterbourne] encountered her in that beautiful abode of flowering desolation known as the Palace of the Caesars. The early Roman spring had filled the air with bloom and perfume, and the rugged surface of the Palatine was muffled with tender verdure. Daisy was strolling along the top of one of those great mounds

of ruin that are embanked with mossy marble and paved with
monumental inscriptions. It seemed to him that Rome had never
been so lovely as just then. He stood looking off at the enchant-
ing harmony of line and colour that remotely encircles the city,
inhaling the softly humid odours and feeling the freshness of the
year and the antiquity of the place reaffirm themselves in mysterious interfusion. It seemed to him also that Daisy had never
looked so pretty; but this had been an observation of his whenever he met her. Giovanelli was at her side, and Giovanelli, too,
wore an aspect of even unwonted brilliancy.

Here Daisy is not identified with a particular society, as she was with the
gay American visitors by the lakeside and in the garden of Vevey, but
simply and wholly with the natural world, which has its own eternal and
beautiful rhythms. Birth is followed by death, and death is followed again
by birth. And the beauty of the natural world—the world to which Daisy
belongs—is supreme. Rome has never been so lovely as when its relics are
"muffled with tender verdure." The monuments of men, the achievements
of civilization, are most beautiful when they are swept again into the round
of natural process. At the moment, Daisy seems to share the natural world,
as she did in the Pincian Garden, with Giovanelli. But at the end of the
nouvelle that "subtle Roman" is quite aware of Daisy's distance even from
himself. He knew, beforehand, that the Colosseum would not be for him,
as it was for Daisy, a "fatal place." "For myself," he says to Winterbourne,
"I had no fear."

Once Daisy is identified with the world of nature, we see that she is
subject to its laws of process. Her very beauty becomes a reminder of her
mortality. So the scene on the Palatine (unlike the scenes at Mrs. Walker's
and on the way to the Pincian Hill) does prepare us effectively for Daisy's
burial in the Protestant cemetery; it does convince us that her death is
inevitable.

III

Yet James's use of his symbolic natural imagery is at once a gain and a
loss. If it solves, almost at the eleventh hour, certain difficulties of tone and
of cause and effect regarding Daisy's death, it also leaves us with some
permanent breaks in the nouvelle's unity of structure. If Daisy is translated
or transfigured in the end into a purely natural ideal of beauty and vitality
and innocence, then what relevance has that ideal to Schenectady, or to

Geneva? If Daisy's death is "fated," does it matter at all what Winterbourne does? And what sort of agent is Giovanelli? Or can we even call him an agent? Hasn't James made inconsequent by the end of his tale, the dramatic conflict—the conflict between two kinds of manners—that he set up in the beginning? The contrast in manners seems to suggest, to hold up as an ideal, a certain way of responding to life. This ideal would combine freedom and vitality with a sophisticated awareness of culture and society. Yet the symbolic imagery of the Palatine Hill seems to elevate natural freedom and vitality and innocence into an ideal so moving, so compelling, that all other considerations pale beside it. Or, if I rephrase my questions about Schenectady and Geneva, Winterbourne and Giovanelli, and answer them in terms of James's creative experience, they come to this: James began writing "Daisy Miller" as a comedy of manners and finished it as a symbolic presentation of a metaphysical ideal. He began by criticizing Daisy in certain ways and ended simply by praising her.

James's friend in the Venetian gondola was, at least in a general way, aware of his transfiguration of Daisy. And James records her opinion—in effect her scolding—in his preface to the New York edition of his nouvelle:

> [Daisy's] only fault is touchingly to have transmuted so sorry a type [as the uncultivated American girl] and to have, by a poetic artifice, not only led our judgement of it astray, but made *any* judgement quite impossible. . . . You *know* you quite falsified, by the turn you gave it, the thing you had begun with having in mind, the thing you had had, to satiety, the chance of "observing": your pretty perversion of it, or your unprincipled mystification of our sense of it, does it really too much honour.

James virtually accepts his friend's criticism. Elsewhere in the preface, speaking in his own voice, he says that, when his nouvelle was first published, the full title ran: "Daisy Miller: A Study." Now, for the New York edition, he subtracts the apposition "in view of the simple truth, which ought from the first to have been apparent to me, that my little exhibition is made to no degree whatever in critical but, quite inordinately and extravagantly, in poetical terms." It appears, then, that James's natural symbolic imagery and his translation of his heroine into a metaphysical figure were unconscious developments. Only after he wrote his nouvelle did James himself discover and acknowledge his own "poetical terms."

Once he had discovered those "terms," he chose to emphasize them, not only in his preface, but also in his text for the New York edition. Viola R. Dunbar has already noted that in a number of places in the final version of "Daisy Miller" James eases his criticism of Daisy and bears down more heavily on the Europeanized Americans. Briefly, he places more stress on Daisy's beauty and innocence, and he associates her more frequently with nature, and more pointedly. At the same time, he gives more asperity to the judgments of Winterbourne and Mrs. Costello and Mrs. Walker. And it is interesting to note as well that James inserts very early in part 1 at least two suggestions of Daisy's final transfiguration. She looks at Winterbourne "with lovely remoteness"; she strikes him as a "charming apparition."

These revisions, though, are occasional and do not essentially change "Daisy Miller." In the New York edition, as well as in the original version, it remains a narrative of imperfect unity, a work that shows unmistakable signs of shifting authorial intention and attitude. And yet, as I have already suggested, James's idealization of his heroine is a matter of gain as well as loss. It resolves certain problems about Daisy's death. More importantly, it adds to the emotional appeal of the second part of the nouvelle. In other words, even if James may have lost something in intellectual consistency by introducing the poetry of Daisy, even if he does to some extent throw away his original comedy of manners, his symbolic natural imagery nonetheless intensifies our response to his story. Again, I return to the articulate lady in the gondola: "As anything charming or touching always to that extent justifies itself, we after a fashion forgive and understand you."

The ideal of a purely natural vitality and freedom and innocence is a strongly, and persistently, attractive ideal. It is attractive, especially, to American writers, and in one variation or another we have, of course, met it before —in Melville, for example, in Hawthorne, in Fitzgerald, in Faulkner. We take James's Daisy Miller, rightly, as prototypical. My purpose here has been to suggest that her relationship to certain major areas of our American experience is even more various than we may previously have thought.

Partial Art—Total Interpretation

Wolfgang Iser

Henry James published "The Figure in the Carpet" in 1896; in retrospect, this short story can be considered as a prognosis for a branch of learning which at the time was barely in its infancy, but which in a relatively short period has fallen increasingly into disrepute. The reference is to that form of interpretation which is concerned first and foremost with the meaning of a literary work. We may assume that Henry James's object was not to make a forecast about the future of literary criticism, and so it follows that in taking the search for meaning as his subject matter, he was dealing with something that was relevant for the reading public of his own time. For, in general, literary texts constitute a reaction to contemporary situations, bringing attention to problems that are conditioned though not resolved by contemporary norms. James's choice of subject shows that conventional means of access to literature must have had their reverse side, and the revelation of this reverse side clearly sheds doubt on the means of access. The implication here is that the search for meaning, which at first may appear so natural and so unconditioned, is in fact considerably influenced by historical norms, even though this influence is quite unconscious. The hypostasis of historical norms, however, has always shown the extent of their inadequacies, and it is this fact that has hastened the demise of this form of literary interpretation. James's short story directly anticipates this demise.

In order to get a more detailed understanding of the problems involved, let us take a closer look at the situation that James deals with in his

From *The Act of Reading*. © 1978 by the Johns Hopkins University Press.

story. The focal point of "The Figure in the Carpet" is the meaning of Vereker's last novel. There are two diverging views of this focal point: that of the first-person narrator, and that of his friend Corvick. Whatever we learn from Corvick's discoveries breaks down against the statements of the first-person narrator. But as Corvick has evidently found what the narrator has been searching for in vain, the reader is bound to resist the orientation of the narrator's perspective. In doing so he will find that the narrator's search for meaning increasingly assumes the proportions of a theme in itself, and finally becomes the object of his, the reader's own, critical attention. This, then, is the situation and the technique.

At the very beginning of the story, the narrator—whom we shall call the critic—boasts that in his review he has revealed the hidden meaning of Vereker's latest novel, and he now wonders how the writer will react to the "loss of his mystery." If interpretation consists in forcing the hidden meaning from a text, then it is only logical to construe the process as resulting in a loss for the author. Now this gives rise to two consequences which permeate the whole story.

First, in discovering the hidden meaning, the critic has, as it were, solved a puzzle, and there is nothing left for him to do but to congratulate himself on this achievement. After all, what can one do with a meaning that has been formulated and put on display, having been stripped of all its mystery? So long as it *was* a mystery, one could search for it, but now there is nothing to arouse interest except for the skill of the searcher. To this the critic would like to draw the attention of his public, which includes Vereker. It is little wonder that he strikes us as a Philistine.

However, this consequence is of minor significance when set beside the second. If the function of interpretation is to extract the hidden meaning from a literary text, this involves certain rather peculiar presuppositions: "If this were so the author, for the sake of future consumption, would disguise a clear meaning which, however, he would keep to himself —and there would also be the following presumption: with the arrival of the critic would come the hour of truth, for he claims to disclose the original meaning together with the reason for its disguise." This brings us to the first guiding (and suspect) norm: If the critic's revelation of the meaning is a loss to the author—as stated at the beginning of the book— then meaning must be a thing which can be subtracted from the work. And if this meaning, as the very heart of the work, can be lifted out of the text, the work is then used up—through interpretation, literature is turned into an item for consumption. This is fatal not only for the text but also for literary criticism, for what can be the function of interpretation if its sole achievement is to extract the meaning and leave behind an empty shell? The parasitic nature of such criticism is all too obvious, which may perhaps give extra force to Vereker's dismissal of the critic's review as the "usual twaddle."

With this judgment Vereker denounces both the archeological ("digging for meaning") approach and the assumption that meaning is a thing which—as is made explicit in the text—embodies a treasure that can be excavated through interpretation. Such a rebuff—uttered by Vereker in the presence of the critic—must inevitably lead to an exposure of the norms that govern interpretation. And here there can be no mistaking their historical nature. The critic defends his initial smugness with the claim that he is searching for truth, and as the truth of the text is a "thing"—which is borne out by the fact that it exists independently of the text—he asks whether Vereker's novel does not contain an esoteric message (which is what he has always supposed in any case), a particular philosophy, basic views of life, or some "extraordinary 'general intention'," or at the very least some stylistic figure impregnated with meaning. Here we have a repertoire of norms that are characteristic of the nineteenth-century concept of literature. For the critic, meaning is to be equated with such norms, and if they are to be extracted from the text as things in themselves, then, clearly, meaning is not something produced by the text. The critic takes this state of affairs so much for granted that one may presume that his expectations must have been shared by most readers of literary works. It seems only natural to the critic that meaning, as a buried secret, should be accessible to and reducible by the tools of referential analysis.

Such analysis sets the meaning in two sorts of a given framework. First, there is the subjective disposition of the critic, i.e., his personal perception, observation, and judgment. He wants to explain the meaning he has discovered. Pontalis, in his discussion of James's short story, has said: "Everything the critics touch goes flat. They want nothing less than to integrate into the general, authorized, established usage a language whose very impetus consists in the fact that it neither could nor would coincide with that usage but must find a style of its own. The critic's modest-seeming explanations as regards his intentions change nothing as regards his procedure; the fact is that he explains, compares, and interprets. These words can drive one mad." Not the least cause of this irritation is the fact that even now literary criticism so frequently proceeds to reduce texts to a referential meaning, despite the fact that this approach has already been persistently questioned, even at the end of the last century.

Nevertheless, there must have been a basic need for the explanation of the meaning of literary works—a need which the critic could fulfill. In the nineteenth century, he had the important function of mediating between work and public in so far as he interpreted the meaning as an orientation for life. This exalted position of the critic and the inlaid link between literature and criticism was explicitly formulated by Carlyle in 1840, with his lectures on *Hero-Worship*; the critic and the man of letters took their places in the Pantheon of the immortals, with the following eulogy: "Men of letters are a perpetual Priesthood, from age to age, teaching all men that a God is still present in their life; that all 'Appearance,' whatsoever we see in the world, is but a vesture for the 'Divine Idea of the World,' for 'that which lies at the bottom of Appearance.' In the true Literary Man there is thus ever, acknowledged or not by the world, a sacredness: he is the light of the world; the world's Priest:—guiding it, like a sacred Pillar of Fire, in its dark pilgrimage through the waste of Time."

This emotional paean, endowing the world with the attributes of God, outlines a principle which for James, just fifty years later, has already become a historic and invalid norm. The critic who reaches behind "Appearance" is, for James, a man reaching into the void. In James's view, appearances are no longer the veil concealing the substance of a meaning; now they are the means to bring into the world something which has never existed at any other time or place before. But so long as the critic's mind is fixed on the hidden meaning, he is incapable—as Vereker tells him—of seeing anything; it is scarcely surprising that ultimately the critic considers the novelist's work to be totally worthless, for it cannot be reduced to the pattern of explanation whose validity the critic never questions. What the reader then has to decide is whether this "worthlessness" applies to Vereker's novel or to the critic's approach.

We may now turn to the second frame of reference that orients the critic. In the nineteenth century, the critic was a man of importance largely because literature promised solutions to problems that could not be solved by the religious, social, or scientific systems of the day. Literature in the nineteenth century, then, was deemed to be of functional importance, for it balanced the deficiencies resulting from systems which all claimed universal validity. In contrast to previous eras, when there had been a more or less stable hierarchy of thought systems, the nineteenth century was lacking in any such stability, owing to the increasing complexity and number of such systems and the resultant clashes between them. These conflicting systems, ranging from theological to scientific, continually encroached on one another's claims to validity, and the importance of fiction as a counterbalance grew in proportion to the deficiencies arising from such conflicts. Literature was able to encompass all existing theories and explanations to an extent that would have been impossible in the previous century, and it was able to offer its solutions wherever these systems reached the limits of their own effectiveness. It was only natural, then, for readers to seek messages in literature, for fiction could offer them precisely the orientation they felt they needed in view of the problems left behind by the various systems of the age. Carlyle's view that "Literature, as far as it is Literature, is an 'apocalypse of Nature,' a revealing of the 'open secret' " was in no way out of the ordinary. The critic in James's novel is also in search of the "open secret," and for him it can only be the message that will ratify the claim of the book to be a work of art.

However, the critic fails—the work does not offer him a detachable message; meaning cannot be reduced to a "thing." The plausible norms of the nineteenth century can no longer function, and the fictional text refuses to be sucked dry and thrown on the rubbish heap.

Now this negation of historical norms is countered by the opposing perspective of Corvick. He seems to have found the "secret," and when he grasps it the effect is so powerful that he cannot find words to express the experience; instead he finds that this experience begins to change his life: "It was immense, but it was simple—it was simple, but it was immense, and the final knowledge of it was an experience quite apart." A series of coincidences prevents the critic from meeting Corvick and learning the reasons for this transformation. And when at last it does seem that they might meet, Corvick falls victim to an accident. Then, like some philological detective, the critic begins to pump Mrs. Corvick and her literary works and, after her death, her second husband—Drayton Deane—in a ceaseless effort to find what he thinks to be the "open secret." But when he finally learns nothing and has to assume that Deane does not know the decoded message of Vereker's novel, he can only console himself by vengefully indicating to Deane that the latter's dead wife must obviously have kept the most important thing from him. The truth-seeker can satisfy his unfulfilled longings by an act of revenge!

But Corvick's discovery is also withheld from the reader, as he is oriented by the perspective of the critic. The result of this is a tension that can only be relieved by the reader's detaching himself from the orientation offered him. This detachment is remarkable, in that normally the reader of fiction accepts the lines laid down for him by the narrator in the course of his "willing suspension of disbelief." Here he must reject such a convention, for this is the only way he can begin to construe the meaning of the novel. Reading, as it were, against the grain is far from easy, for the presumptions of the critic—i.e., that meaning is a message or a philosophy of life—seem so natural that they are still adhered to even today. Indeed, the reaction to modern art is still that same old question: "What's it supposed to mean?" Now if the reader is to reject the perspective of the critic, the implication is that he must read against his own prejudices, but the readiness to do so can only be brought about by making the critic's perspective responsible for withholding what the reader wishes to know. The process then consists of the reader gradually realizing the inadequacy of the perspective offered him, turning his attention more and more to that which he had up to now been taking for granted, and finally becoming aware of his own prejudices. The "willing suspension of disbelief" will then apply, not to the narrative framework set up by the author, but to those ideas that had hitherto oriented the reader himself. Ridding oneself of such prejudices—even if only temporarily—is no simple task.

The large-scale withholding of information about the secret uncovered by Corvick sharpens the reader's perception to the extent that he cannot avoid noting the signals that permeate the vain search for meaning. The most important one is given the critic by Vereker himself, although unlike Corvick he fails to understand it: "For himself, beyond doubt, the thing we were all so blank about was vividly there. It was something, I guessed, in the primal plan, something like a complex figure in a Persian carpet. He highly approved of this image when I used it, and he used another himself. 'It's the very string,' he said, 'that my pearls are strung on'!" Instead of being able to grasp meaning like an object, the critic is confronted by an empty space. And this emptiness cannot be filled by a single referential meaning, and any attempt to reduce it in this way leads to nonsense. The critic himself gives the key to this different quality of meaning, which James also underlines by calling his story "The Figure in the Carpet," and which Vereker confirms in the presence of the critic: meaning is imagistic in character. This was the direction Corvick had taken right from the start. He tells the critic, ". . . there was more in Vereker than met the eye," to which the critic can only reply: "When I remarked that the eye seemed what the printed page had been expressly invented to meet he immediately accused me of being spiteful because I had been foiled."

The critic, working with unstinting philological pains, never gives up his attempt to find a meaning that is precisely formulated on the printed page. And so he sees nothing but blanks which withhold from him what he is seeking in vain on that printed page. But the formulated text, as Vereker and Corvick understand it, represents a pattern, a structured indicator to guide the imagination of the reader; and so the meaning can only be grasped as an image. The image provides the filling for what the textual pattern structures but leaves out. Such a "filling" represents a basic condition of communication, but although Vereker actually names this mode of communication, the allusion has no effect on the critic, because for him meaning can only become meaning if it can be grasped within a frame of reference. The image cannot be related to any such frame, for it does not represent something that exists; on the contrary, it brings into existence something that is to be found neither outside the book nor on its printed pages. However, the critic cannot follow this thought through, and if he did accept what Vereker says, in respect of meaning being revealed in an imaginary picture, it would be because at best he envisaged such a picture as the image of a given reality, which must exist independently before any such process can get under way.

But it is absurd to imagine something with which one is already confronted. The critic, however, cannot see this, and so he remains blind to the difference between image and discourse as two independent concepts that cannot be reduced to one. His approach is characterized by the division between subject and object which always applies to the acquisition of knowledge; here the meaning is the object, which the subject attempts to define in relation to a particular frame of reference. The fact that this frame is (apparently) independent of the subject is what constitutes the criterion for the truthfulness of the definition. However, if meaning is imagistic in character, then inevitably there must be a different relationship between text and reader from that which the critic seeks to create through his referential approach. Such a meaning must clearly be the product of an interaction between the textual signals and the reader's acts of comprehension. And, equally clearly, the reader cannot detach himself from such an interaction; on the contrary, the activity stimulated in him will link him to the text and induce him to create the conditions necessary for the effectiveness of that text. As text and reader thus merge into a single situation, the division between subject and object no longer applies, and it therefore follows that meaning is no longer an object to be defined, but is an effect to be experienced.

This is the situation which James thematizes through the perspective of Corvick. After he has experienced the meaning of Vereker's novel, his life is changed. But all he can do is report this extraordinary change—he cannot explain or convey the meaning as the critic seeks to do. This change also affects Mrs. Corvick, who after her husband's death embarks on a new literary venture which disappoints the critic in so far as he cannot work out the influences that might enable him to discover the hidden meaning of Vereker's novel.

It may be that James has exaggerated the effect of the literary work, but whatever one's opinions may be in this respect, there can be no doubt that he has given a very clear account of two totally different approaches to the fictional text. Meaning as effect is a perplexing phenomenon, and such perplexity cannot be removed by explanations—on the contrary, it invalidates them. The effectiveness of the work depends on the participation of the reader, but explanations arise from (and also lead to) detachment; they will therefore dull the effect, for they relate the given text to a given frame of reference, thus flattening out the new reality brought into being by the fictional text. In view of the irreconcilability of effect and explanation, the traditional expository style of interpretation has clearly had its day.

A Reading of "The Real Thing"

Moshe Ron

> *Artifice que la réalité, bon à fixer l'intellect moyen entre les mirages d'un fait, mais elle repose par cela même sur quelque universelle entente . . .*
>
> STÉPHANE MALLARMÉ

> *Henry James was, I may truthfully say, the only sitter who ever terrified me.*
>
> ALICE BOUGHTON
(who photographed him in 1906)

> *The phantoms of their brains have gained mastery over them.*
>
> The German Ideology

It is by the very Jamesian principle of economy of representation that "The Real Thing" recommends itself to us for treatment. We wish to describe how a James story *works*, as well as to probe some of the difficult questions with which "the art of representation bristles." The aim being double, and relations stopping nowhere, the problem is to draw by some geometry (we dare not call it our own) "the circle within which they shall *appear* to do so." Here this short story plays into our hands; for it declares itself to be structured like a chiasmus while at the same time dramatizing thematically the problem of representation itself. As the locus of this coincidence, "The Real Thing" is obliging almost to the point of converting our stated difficulty into its opposite: its very explicitness threatens to eliminate the possibility of a critical game. We are thus forced to confront yet another more awesome problem: that of our own interpretative activity and its relation to the text.

From *Yale French Studies* no. 58 (1979). © 1979 by *Yale French Studies*.

I

The rhetorical space of the story is constituted by two polarities: master/slave and art/life. This space is called "the studio"; it is a magic place where life (the flesh and blood model) is converted into art (the illustration in black and white): while along the other axis, the slave (the cockney, the foreign street-vendor) becomes master (the English aristocrats Rutland Ramsay and Artemisia). Professionalism is the name of the dynamic element within this field, the amateurish representing the opposite principle of inertia. The agent of this double transformation is the artist, who also participates in another apparently less magic transaction whereby the professional skill of the model is exchanged for the economic power represented by money. The degree of mastery thus earned is safely contained within the system, since it does not change the fundamental hierarchy in the studio.

The system we have tried to describe thus smoothly operating surrounds and underlies the story, that is to say, it is not the story itself. It is in fact the non-story, the other of the story which constitutes it: only with the normal circulation within the studio *jammed*—the obstacle being the Monarchs—is the possibility of the story *opened*. The story may thus be likened to a game which consists in breaking its own rules. An extra-textual excursion to the available "before" and "after" of "The Real Thing"—a notebook entry from February 22, 1891, and a paragraph from the preface to volume 18 of the New York edition—may lend support to this paradoxical assertion. As related by George du Maurier, the anecdote —the "germ" of the story as James calls it—concerned only "an oldish ruined pair—he an officer in the army—who unable to turn a penny in any other way, were trying to find employment as models." This initial *donnée* generates the norm to which the eventual Monarchs are the exception: "Let my contrast and my complication here come from the opposition —to my melancholy Major and his wife—of a couple of little vulgar professional people who *know*, with the consequent bewilderment, vagueness, depression of the former . . . their failure, disappointment, disappearance—going forth into the vague again." We juxtapose this pre-textual fragment with the later preface, in which the origin is narrated as follows:

> In like manner my much loved friend George du Maurier had spoken to me of a call from a strange and striking couple desirous to propose themselves as artist's models for his weekly "social" illustrations to "Punch," and the acceptance of whose

services would have entailed the dismissal of an undistinguished but highly expert pair, also husband and wife, who had come to him from far back on the irregular day and whom, thanks to a happy, and to that extent lucrative, appearance of "type" on the part of each, he had reproduced, to the best effect in a thousand drawing-room attitudes and combinations.

The story of the strange couple must be represented as a snag in the art-producing machine whose invention precisely for that purpose is recorded in the *Notebooks*. By the time of the preface, the system seems to have been in operation from time immemorial; the image of the happy studio recedes into the pre-history of the original anecdote—James in the interval having "forgotten" that this nature had been engendered by the story. (Not that he always forgot: the preface to *The Portrait of a Lady* states the storyteller's problem to be that of "positively organizing an ado about Isabel Archer," thus restoring the cart to its original place before the horses.)

The opposite relation between artist and model, obtained at the cost of reversing the flow of cash, is inherent in the situation of the fashionable portrait painter (a title which the artist of our text prizes over that of an illustrator). In a system thus constituted, some difficulties may be foreseen: the professionalism of the artist will have to compensate for its lack in the model; the artist will have lost his position of absolute authority in the studio. But the possibility of a portrait-producing system, if not realized in the story's *action*, is nevertheless necessary for its *narration*. When a "gentleman and a lady" are announced, those linguistic signs evoke immediately an erroneous "vision of sitters." With the Monarchs, two sentences later, physically present in the studio, the narrative states that "there was nothing at first to indicate that they mightn't have come for a portrait." We may be warranted in recognizing here the most elementary narrative device: the error and promise of its demystification—the temporal deployment of a duplicitous sign. The narrative introduces a sign which is subsequently revealed to have been a question (here: what kind of sitters are the Monarchs?) and proceeds to give the right answer (they come as paid models), but not before offering the wrong one (they come as patrons) and three of its unrealized ramifications (cf. the last three sentences of the second paragraph). The text then plays on a linguistic form which may function equally well in either of the systems now competing for inclusion in the story and thus most resembles this particular instance of error: the verb "to pay" as used by the Major ("We should like to make it pay") summarizes the situation, for despite its active form, it is neither active nor passive, having for a subject a strictly grammatical non-referential "it," and discreetly forbidding combination with a named object.

If the system consisting of the polarities master/slave and art/life provides the thematic basis for the story, a third polarity, which we might name sign/meaning (or, according to the needs of our exposition, appearance/reality, form/force, outside/inside, etc.), gives it its temporal, properly narrative dimension.

The question which the narrative now asks is: can the Monarchs sit for *Rutland Ramsay*? A positive answer is suggested by the common sense notion of their aptness for the job in being "the real thing." The artist's doubt, deriving from his theory of art, materializes eventually into a negative answer. But the singularity, the interest of the narrative game, we don't mind repeating, is the simultaneity with which it makes and breaks its rules. Thus it is only after it has been ascertained that the Monarchs pretend to make part of the illustration-producing system that the picture of this system is completed. The missing elements, Miss Churm and Oronte, when introduced create a formal symmetry (they are the opposite of the Monarchs both in quality and in number) which is also a thematic redundancy (there are too many models in the studio). The question proposed a few lines higher may then be reformulated as: *who* shall sit for *Rutland Ramsay*? The answer to this question is temporally enacted as a *struggle*.

This is rendered by adding to the main function of the employees in the studio, that of sitting, the subsidiary one of serving tea. The assignment of these functions to the various agents indicates the hierarchy within the studio; the inversion of roles signifies a reversal of this hierarchy. First it is Miss Churm, who in the presence of the "other sitters" is asked "to be so good as to lend a hand in getting tea." A turning point is reached when, while Oronte is sitting, Mrs. Monarch is asked "if she would mind laying it out." Within the sitting function there are two distinctions: sitting for the Cheapside magazine is lower than doing the same for a connoisseur's novel like *Rutland Ramsay*; sitting for "the low life of the book"—as the Monarchs suppose Miss Churm to be doing, and as the artist does not dare to ask the Major to do—is obviously less prestigious than being represented as aristocrats. More significant are the gradations within the other function: they help situate its performer with exactitude within the polarity master/slave. There is serving tea to the artist, which is one thing, and serving it to the model, which is another. Thus Miss Churm, on the following visit, accuses the artist of "having wished to humiliate her," and the Monarchs are said to feel "as if they were waiting on [his] servant." Another nuance is marked between performing this service occasionally, upon special request and under the guise of a friendly gesture on the one hand, and doing it regularly and as a paid duty on the other. The last action of the Monarchs ("they washed my crockery, they put it away") is a still intenser version of this function. The narrator's interpretation of this act announces the end of the struggle and explicitly names the structure we have been trying so painstakingly to describe in operation: "If my servants were models, then my models might be my servants. They would reverse the parts—the others would sit for the ladies and gentlemen and *they* would to the work." In fact, Oronte had already taken his drink from Mrs. Monarch "*as if* he had been a gentleman at a party squeezing a crush hat under his elbow (my italics), and Miss Churm was said, on the occasion of her serving tea, to have "tried intonations—*as if* she too wished to pass for the real thing" (my italics). This recurrent "as if" permits the narrative to make the symmetry and subsequent reversal more complete without regard to historical or psychological verisimilitude (norms which it is otherwise loath to violate). Rhetorically the final inversion may be considered as the simple elimination of such earlier *as ifs*.

The formal symmetry having been demonstrated, the narrative can now resolve the thematic redundancy. Led by its own logic, the story of the Monarchs asks a last question: can they be servants in the studio? After a feeble gesture towards the affirmative ("I pretended I could, to oblige them, for about a week"), the question is dismissed with a negative answer. Their briefly reported departure is followed by the system's "return" to smooth operation ("I obtained the remaining books").

II

The interest of the Monarchs' story derives at least in part from the superficial logic of their move. "They had reasoned out their opportunity" since the artist is charged with representing contemporary gentlefolk, it naturally makes sense that the opportunity to use real specimens of that class would facilitate his task. "Wouldn't it be rather a pull sometime to have—a to have—?" the Major asks "awkwardly," "the *real* thing, a gentleman you know, or a lady," and the artist, his theoretical preferences notwithstanding, is "quite ready to give general assent." A first encounter with their competition for the job results in their going off "with increase of comfort, founded on their *demonstrable* advantage in being the real thing" (my italics).

Before we're done with the Monarchs, we shall have to submit their "reality" to a more rigorous scrutiny. If we provisionally take them at their word, the message of the story appears to be a demystification of a current error in aesthetic theory. The currency of the error may be ascribed most plausibly to the late nineteenth century (Realism, Naturalism) or else to certain bad artists at various periods or to philistines at all times. From this viewpoint the polarity art/life is brought to the foreground at the expense of the one we initially called master/slave. Such a reading is briefly stated in a current survey of James: " 'The Real Thing' (1892) ironically states the idea that Impressionism is a sounder principle of creative art than literal Realism."

There is no need to question here the aptness of such terms (migrant terminology from art history abounds in James's criticism) for the text defines the contrast and states its preference quite explicitly:

> [The Monarchs] saw a couple of other drawings that I had made of [Oronte], and Mrs. Monarch hinted that it never would have struck her that he had sat for them. "Now the drawings you made from *us*, they look exactly like us," she reminded me, smiling in triumph; and I recognized that this was indeed just their defect. When I drew the Monarchs I couldn't anyhow get away from them—get into the character I wanted to represent; and I hadn't the least desire my model should be discoverable in my picture.

The criterion by which common sense judges art is faithfulness to reality. It takes photography as its model for art in general. The Monarchs consider their experience with that art as an asset. "We've been photographed— *immensely*," says Mrs. Monarch on the first visit; she proves "capable of remaining for an hour almost as motionless as before a photographer's lens," and the resultant drawing "looks like a photograph or a copy of a photograph." Photography is a still, not to say a dead art.

To this we can oppose the artist's semi-joking plea to "allow for the alchemy of art." The allusion, buried in the cliché, to an art exposed by modern science as superstition of fraud, makes it a particularly apt contrast to photography, so characteristic a product of the positivist age. The artist knows that the successful exercise of his art consists in transforming and not merely in copying his model. The insertion of the real into the process has the effect of a short circuit. It brings together poles which ought to stay apart, such as the model and the personage he is supposed to represent: " 'Oh I'm not a Russian princess,' Mrs. Monarch protested a little coldly. I could see she had known some and didn't like them. There was at once a complication of a kind I never had to fear with Miss Churm." Having had the leisure "to sketch a little" themselves, the Monarchs may prove " 'artistic'—which would be a great complication." Even if not for these specifically feared "complications," working with them as models amounts to a reversal of the normal order: "I found myself trying to invent types that approached her [Mrs. Monarch's] own, instead of making her own transform itself." This is neither the only nor the first such reversal involving the Monarchs.

If "character" is the name given to the artist's success in capturing the essence of his subject, extracting the inner truth from an outward appearance, "type" is the opposite: it is the model recognizable in the canvas, the appearance merely reproduced. The narrator is quite emphatic about his preference: "the thing in the world I most hated was being ridden by a type"; "I held that everything was to be sacrificed sooner than character." "Type"—the Monarchs as models—is often combined with metaphors of incarceration, pursuit or domination: "I couldn't anyhow get away from them"; "being ridden by a type"; "servitude to a type"; "obsessional form." That these figures are not innocent—not mere figures of speech—is a point to which we shall have to return.

While Miss Churm's performance was "simply suggestive," "a word to the wise," the Monarchs, with all their reserve, are all too talkative an image. Like Mrs. Anstruther-Thompson at Lady Lindsay's dinner, they tell too much:

> There had been but ten words [wrote James in the preface to *The Spoils of Poynton*], yet I had recognized in them all the possibilities of the little drama of my "spoils," which glimmered there and then into life: so that when in the next breath I began to hear of the action taken. . . I saw clumsy life again at her stupid work. For the action taken. . . I had absolutely, and could have, no scrap of use; one had been so perfectly qualified to say in advance: "It's the perfect little workable thing, but she'll strangle it in the cradle, even while she pretends all so cheeringly to rock it; wherefore I'll stay her hand while yet there's time. "I didn't, of course, stay her hand—there never is in such cases "time"; and I had once more the full demonstration of the fatal futility of Fact.

Whereas the Monarchs are "already made," "the value of such a model as Miss Churm resided precisely in the fact that she had no positive stamp." The Monarchs act as a full sign, in which signifier, signified and referent are bound necessarily and permanently, and which even in reproduction continues to stand for itself: they are "the real thing, but always the same thing." This is poor economy. The valuable model is in itself utterly non-referential; it is susceptible of being inserted successively in different codes so as to stand for each one of them in its entirety. Miss Churm as the Russian princess with the Golden Eyes looks "distinguished and charming, foreign and dangerous." Oronte opens the door for Mrs. Monarch "standing there with the rapt pure gaze of the young Dante spellbound by the young Beatrice." "When I put him into some old clothes of my own he looked like an Englishman. He was as good as Miss Churm, who could look, when requested, like an Italian." The Monarchs cannot look anything but their age (James made a point of not making them much older than their rivals), and are reluctant to appear in any clothes but their own. It is Miss Churm's "pride to feel that she could sit for characters that had nothing in common with each other," while their pride is to remain what they are even in adversity. It is "odd" how "being so little in herself she could be so much in others"; but this non-adequation of sign and meaning is good economy, yielding much (in art) for little (in life), ensuring the economic and aesthetic rentability of the studio's operation.

By repeatedly declaring its preference for variety of expression over sameness, character over type, the ideal over the real thing, etc., the text asks us to read it as a demystification. But here the argument begins to turn against itself and compels us to demystify the demystification. Strictly speaking, rejected from the beginning in theory—and then illustrated in the narrated action—is the notion that the model *must* be the real thing or that there is an *advantage* for art in its being so. But why *can't* the real thing be a model? (This question is not entirely absent from the text. When Hawley puts the blame on the models' being "stupid," the artist's reply is: "You mean *I* am—for I ought to get round that.")

The referential validity of the "real thing" proves not to be a satisfactory explanation. This is indicated by a closer examination of what is here given this name. If we ask ourselves: what is the reality of the Monarchs? What is their essence, or in what sense are they an essence? The curious answer is that their essence is *appearance*. Without possessing any of the economic and political power which is the essence of the upper class, they *represent* this class to perfection in their speech, their manners, their clothes. Their appearance acts as a powerful sign ("It is odd how quickly I was sure of everything that concerned them"), suggestive of the entire semantic field of English aristocratic life, described with extraordinary rhetorical *élan* in the first two paragraphs of the story's part 2. The verbs "fancy," "see," "imagine," "evoke," still indicating awareness of the dubiously referential character of the description in the first paragraph, are dropped in the second; even while being uttered the cliché acquires the convincingness of reality. Commenting on Mrs. Monarch's appearance the narrator says: "Her husband had used the word that described her: she was in the London current jargon 'smart.' Her figure was, in the same order of ideas, conspicuously and irreproachably, 'good'." Here is an instance of what Jakobson calls overlapping of message and code: The text simply tells us how to read Mrs. Monarch, not allowing our unfamiliarity with the specific code (by now obsolete) to stand in the way. Just before the first scene which marks their defeat "they came in, the Major and his wife, with their society laugh about nothing (there was less and less to laugh at); came in like country-callers—they always reminded one of that—who have walked across the park after church and are presently persuaded to stay to luncheon." The disparity between what is evoked in the narrator's mind and the actual situation reveals the Monarchs as no more than coded signs without the least referential value. In fact what begins to claim our interest is the vividness and detail of the allusion, the tenacity of the code in face of empirical reality, its continued operation as a sign for that which is not.

Even the name "Major Monarch"—with its elegant alliteration, the title alluding to a martial past (an allusion never substantiated by the minutest detail) and the semantic presence of the institution of royalty—is a blatant over-statement: what could be real enough to keep the promise of such a name? The appearance of the Monarchs is misleading: they look as if they have ten thousand a year, while in reality are seeking a poorly paying job. When this error is demystified the narrative comes to a provisional rest ("It was only then that I understood") with the statement of a non-adequation between inside and outside, although the healing virtue of this realization is made somewhat questionable by the narrator's earlier claim that this "paradoxical law" has not been unsuspected from the start ("I have been for some time conscious that a figure with a good deal of frontage was, as one might say, almost never a public institution"). The pathos of the story, its "depth," is dependent upon the impression that this non-adequation is merely *accidental* (the Major: "we've had the misfortune to lose our money"; the narrator: "at present something had happened—it didn't matter what").

But it is not only that the Monarchs behave or that the narrator reads their behavior according to a code that is inappropriate to the specific situation—although the text explicitly communicates both these effects;

the code of "society" itself is declared from the beginning to have the status of fiction: the advantages of the would-be models strike the artist as "preponderantly social; such for instance as would help to make a drawing-room look well. However, *a drawing-room was always, or ought to be, a picture*" (my italics). Mrs. Monarch's premarital nickname of "the Beautiful Statue" fits well into this picture. "When she stood erect she took naturally one of the attitudes in which court painters represent queens and princesses." And later in the story, the Monarchs resemble "a pair of patient courtiers in a royal ante-chamber."

The real thing then is already an artifact in its original habitat. But what is a drawing-room the picture of?

A drawing-room, the "social" code in general, signifies *prosperity*. This should help us to grasp the anomaly that gives rise to the story; as James put it in his notebook,

> the pathos, the oddity, the typicalness of the situation—the little tragedy of good-looking gentlefolk, who had been all their lives stupid and well-dressed . . . like so many of their class in England, and were now utterly unable to *do* anything, had no cleverness, no art or craft to make use of as a *gagne-pain*—could only *show* themselves, clumsily, for the fine, clean, well groomed animals that they were, only hoping to make a little money by—in this manner—just simply being.

The effect of oddity seems to stem from the metonymic reversal implicit in the Monarchs' offering of their services as models. Their doing so reveals them as pure *form*, without any of the *force* such form is normally supposed to represent. The paraphernalia of aristocracy which they exemplify to perfection are, after all, the sanctions of a certain social status, privileges ultimately derived from success in some prehistorical (having occurred in an earlier history or simply before the beginning of the story) struggle for economic and political power. It is only later, so to speak, and at the cost of forgetting the original causal relation, that the form is taken to *represent* the force which created it, even and especially in the absence of such force. In the Monarchs this reversal is completed: "their good looks had been their capital." Not only in the studio, but even in the drawing-room, prior to their obscure disaster, the Monarchs wish to turn their appearance and manners, which are an effect—and a side effect at that—into the cause of economic prosperity. Other Jamesian narratives retell in various ways this curious exchange of forms for money (force needs form as much as form needs force) and this is perhaps the elementary structure of his fiction.

The wide ideological gap which makes such manoeuvres possible may seem as symptomatic of late nineteenth-century English society. James's notebook entry quoted above likens the couple to "so many of their class in England"; and for the artist's friend Hawley "they were a compendium of everything he most objected to in the social system of his country." This is as close as we come to the nausea which in literature often follows the discovery of the non-adequation inside/outside in history (e.g., in *Hamlet*). In such a reading, the oddity of the Monarchs is enlarged and transferred by synecdoche to an entire social class in a given historical period. The non-coincidence of force and form—especially when accompanied with blind faith in the latter—may be read as the sign of an aged culture, of decadence in general. But let not those typicalities mask an even more general one: both the symptom (the Monarchs' case) and the diagnosis (anachronism of aristocratic ideology in nineteenth-century England, aging of civilization) we produced for it, point not only to an accident of history, a specific cultural illness—they do that too—but also to the congenitality of the illness that is culture: its semiotic nature (as it were) that opens the possibility of history, of any narrative (including the present one).

We seem to have gone very far out of our way—perhaps too far— but once we began there was no stopping. In the process we have levelled off some of the differences that might be taken to account for the preferences manifested by the text. The ground for rejecting the Monarchs in favor of their plebeian rivals cannot be the ontological authority of either: a careful reading reveals such authority to be generally undermined. Nor can it be a greater or a smaller gap between inside and outside: this non-adequation characterizes both pairs of models, and is not, as such, valorized one way or another. Moreover, the text itself declares the irrelevancy of such criteria, and at a rather early stage, when the artist describes what he terms his "perversity," "an innate preference for the represented subject over the real one: the defect of the real one was so apt to be a lack of representation. I liked things that appeared; then one was sure. Whether they *were* or not was a subordinate and almost always profitless question."

It would seem as though the harder we look the more difficult it becomes to find a *reason* for the text's preference: our investigation only reasserts more forcefully the rigorous symmetry between the two pairs of models. One of the paradoxes is that while in statements such as we have just quoted the Monarchs are suspected of "lack of representation," their failure as models is later attributed to a sort of *excess*. The advantage of Miss Churm, let us recall, is a lack of any positive stamp; in fact the less determined the model, the more suitable it is. The "detestation of the amateur," which the narrator proclaims to be "the ruling passion of [his] life," turns out to be not a rejection of an absent in favor of a present quality, but rather the opposite: professional know-how, the positive point of the model is manifested as a negativity. The chiasmus is a double-crossing: the vacant aristocratic face, which is a full sign, is exchanged for an empty sign, which the artist and the model between them, know how to fill with expression. (Note also that the name "Churm" is almost an anagram of "Monarch").

If the conflict is, as it appears to be, between two figural modes of representation, these are distinguishable only by their intentionality: to some extent it is an attitude towards one's being a sign (one's own rhetoricity, to use De Man's term) which is here valorized. The Monarchs as a signifier claim a necessary and historical continuity with the signified. Signification in that case would resemble a metaphor (they are one pair of aristocrats standing for another pair of aristocrats) and, in a second remove, a synecdoche (inasmuch as Rutland Ramsay stands for Aristocracy in general). Let us recall, however, that the structure of the Monarchs as a literary sign emerged from our previous discussion looking more like a metonymy (effect for cause). *The Monarchs then are a metonymy trying to pass for a metaphor.* The professional models, on the other hand, claim no continuity with what they are supposed to represent, or if they do, their claim is so manifestly unfounded that the artist does not have to take it seriously. Their figural mode is essentially discontinuous: the intention which gives them meaning is not inherent in them but derives entirely from the artist in the process of representation. In fact it is required of them, as we have mentioned earlier, to be ignorant of Russian princesses on the one hand and of the mysteries of draftsmanship on the other. But if this is so then they too can have no awareness of the rhetorical structure of their role. Conversely, the Monarchs fulfill the requirement of ignorance equally well: having presumably read *Rutland Ramsay*, they failed to notice the absence of low life scenes in the novel and so the symmetry reasserts itself once more. If it is *their* intention that prevails, perhaps it is in the artist that an explanation must be sought; for we ought not to have forgotten that it takes *two* to make a sign function.

III

We have talked so far as if the only subject of the story were the Monarchs. Like any other Jamesian text, "The Real Thing" here forces upon us the question posed in the preface to *The Reverberator*: "Of whom, when it comes to the point, is the fable narrated?" The fable we are here concerned with is of the narrating as much as of the narrated subject; to be more precise, it is about the way one subject interprets another, thereby constituting or failing to constitute itself. The emphasis thus shifts to the narrator himself, and the question may be raised whether his interpretation of the Monarchs does them justice.

The vocabulary of coercion, as we have intimated, is not only a figure: it is neither accidental nor innocent. For the magic operation of the studio, a certain monopoly by the artist is an indispensable prerequisite. The artist wants the model to be an histrion who can assume different postures, masks, roles, an empty figure waiting to be filled, a marionette, in short, a non-person: the model must above all not presume to take himself seriously. The Monarchs won't do because they refuse to play games or wear clothes not their own, because they are self-respecting people who take themselves seriously. It is not by chance that in the model the function of serving—whatever benign or ritual aspects it might take—coincides with that of sitting. The *morality* of this arrangement is dubious; the artist who instituted it (and who, by attempting to mask it, betrays himself) is a Boothian Unreliable Narrator through and through. Thus a recent critic wrote:

> In "The Real Thing" the narrator justifies himself for his failure with the Monarchs—shifting the blame to them. . . .
>
> One of the primary—and most subtle—motivations in the story is to bring about what is finally demonstrated in the final scene of the Monarchs in the story—their serving him in the capacity of menials. In a way this is what he has been after through the story, to bring them down a few pegs, almost to find a scapegoat for what he somehow must recognize as his own inadequacies.
>
> (David Toor, "Narrative Irony in Henry James' 'The Real Thing.' ")

The narrator, then, is untruthful; aggression is on his side; the Monarchs are victimized, "almost" scapegoated (no blood is spilled); the notion that they exercise some power on him must be a subsequent rationalization of an unmanly act of violence. Our acceptance of this notion hitherto is perhaps a symptom of our own inadequacies. It seems as though one must either scapegoat or be scapegoated by the text (there is an undeniable pleasure in it whichever way it goes); which makes one wonder whether interpretation is not always an act of violence, the act of violence *par excellence*.

The unreliability of the narrator is manifested in the insincerity of his attitude towards the Monarchs. He claims to like them ("they were so simple") and often refers to them as his "friends." He is *entertained* by them, and the ambiguity of this word, the connotations of condescension, amusement at their expense, downright exploitation, occasionally come to the surface: "to hear [the Major] talk was to combine the excitement of going out with the economy of staying at home"; and a few lines down: "he hadn't a stray sixpence of an idea to fumble for." This note is struck as soon as the artist is acquainted with the meaning of the Monarch's appearance in his studio:

> I was so amused by them, that to get more of it, I did my best to take their point of view; and though it was an embarrassment to find myself appraising physically, as if they were animals on hire or useful blacks, a pair whom I should have expected to meet only in one of the relations in which criticism is tacit, I looked at Mrs. Monarch judicially enough to be able to exclaim after a moment with conviction: "Oh yes, a lady in a book!" She was singularly like a bad illustration.

The amusement is here paid for—verbally, at least—with embarrassment. But what credibility can the narrator's "judiciality" and "conviction" have, when the exclamation of his approval is immediately followed by a tacit disparagement? Perhaps the conditional is misleading and this is after all "a situation in which criticism is tacit." Is it the narrator's intention to play with the Monarchs by hiding from them the truth, or is there something in them which forbids criticism? Why is the narrator "as reassuring as [he] knew how to be," when "somehow with all their perfections [he] didn't easily believe in them"? "The comfortable *candour* which now prevailed between us" looks dubious in the light of the admission, two sentences later, that "I postponed a little *timidly* perhaps the solving of my question" (my italics). On the following page the notion that this hesitation has anything to do with any intimidation by the Monarchs is vigorously denied: "If I went a little in fear of them it wasn't because they bullied me, because they had got an oppressive foothold." [Elsewhere] the narrator is almost grateful for the non-violence of the Major: "So earnest a desire to please was touching in a man who could so easily have knocked one down."

We could quote other passages but we might as well stop here: the man protests too much. It is hard to tell whether the artist's fear of the Monarchs is made possible by forgetting their unreality, or whether the doubts cast on their reality are meant to repress a real danger emanating from them (in this "forgetting" the critic must participate as much as the narrator). In our judgment the inconsistency of the narrator's attitude is the sign not simply of his insincerity but of a real contradiction. The presence of the Monarchs acts as a threat, yet their aggression is denied, the desire to see them go is covered up, the inescapable confrontation is postponed as long as possible. When the word "Oh my dear Major—I can't be ruined for you!" is finally said, self-castigation follows immediately: "It was a horrid speech." Compare the "latent eloquence" of the Monarchs and its effect on the narrator with his easy dismissal of Miss Churm's vocal accusation that he wished to humiliate her ("she hadn't resented the outrage at the time."). An early use of emotional language—"It was going to wring tears from me, I felt, the way she hid her head, ostrich-like, in the other broad bosom"—should probably be understood ironically; but a later show of feeling in reaction to the Monarchs' dish-washing act—"I confess that my drawing was blurred for a moment—the picture swam"—is surely meant to come across as sincere. Some of the words used on that occasion even have a religious flavor: the other sitters are said to be "also evidently mystified and awestruck." It is just when the Monarchs prepare to assume the role of servants that the narrator talks of "one of the most *heroic* personal services" and of "*noble* humility" in relation to Mrs. Monarchs's actions (my italics). In other words it is at the point of maximum distance from the essence of Aristocracy that they are credited with the attributes of that essence. We recognize in this strange mixture of anxiety and fascination, aggression and guilt—the word is used here in its vaguest and most general sense—an Oedipal situation.

Without claiming too much for the allusion let us mention that James "thought of representing the husband as jealous of the wife—that is of the artist employing her, from the moment that, in point of fact she begins to sit. But this is vulgar and obvious—worth nothing." This possibility momentarily worries the narrator ("the idea was too worrisome") and is then dismissed ("I soon saw there was nothing in it"); "I judged rightly that in their awkward situation their close union was their main comfort and that this union had no weak spot. It was a real marriage, an encouragement to the hesitating, a nut for pessimists to crack." Perhaps "reality" is always like a marriage, an alliance from which one is condemned to remain excluded. What is being said here implicitly is: even if I wanted I wouldn't have a chance. If it were our intention to spin a psychoanalytic fable we might construe this affirmation of the Major's safe possession of his wife and idealization of their marriage as a clue to some undealt with Oedipus complex. Incidentally, while George Du Maurier, the original subject of the anecdote, was in his late fifties at the time, probably older than the models and in any case an established and successful artist, James made his narrator younger than his models and deprived him of the assurance brought by public recognition. At such a distance from the common-sense surface of the text, some buried associations of the name "Monarch" come to life (only ruler, single origin), and the title "Major" literally recovers its comparative value: "Arrange as I would and take the precautions I would [Mrs. Monarch] always came out, in my pictures, too tall—landing me in the dilemma of having represented a fascinating woman as seven feet high, which (out of respect perhaps to my own very much scantier inches) was far from my idea of such a personage. The case was worse with the Major —nothing I could do would keep *him* down." If an artist's work is, in a sense, a representation of himself, the aggrandized figures of the models become the measure of the belittling of that self. Thus Hawley, the painter's friend, tosses back the drawings "with visible irreverence," pronouncing them "execrable, given the sort of thing [the narrator] represented [himself] as wishing to arrive at."

Hélène Cixous has written admirably well of the ambiguous way in which littleness functions in James:

> *Little*, vocable propitiatoire, suggère en l'auteur une attitude défensive, penchée, délicate, à laquelle il ne faut pas se fier: c'est que little (petit, jeune) est l'écran fragile de son contraire. . . . A la limite il faudrait interroger toute manifestation de faiblesse (jeunesse de Maisie, maladie de Ralph Touchette ou Milly Theale, bêtise de Catherine Sloper, pauvreté de Kate Croy, d'Osmond) au risque de s'y laisser prendre. On y décèlerait facilement les plus grandes forces, celles justement qui sont les points de résistance ou d'agression de réel.

The narrator of "the Real Thing" falls into the same pattern. The literal dissymmetry he claims to exist between him and the Monarchs ("my own very much scantier inches") only masks—and thereby reveals to the attentive reader—a very real symmetry (*their* weakness being a shortage of money and brains). The obvious symmetry between the two pairs of models is, as we have mentioned earlier, necessary for the narration of the story; the one, more implicit, which we are discussing now functions at the level of action. This symmetry, like the other is more of a redundancy than an equilibrium: there are too many masters in the studio (and too many victims in the story).

Symmetry is the condition of possibility for chiasmus. And indeed the relation between the artist and his aristocratic models takes the seesaw form of this rhetorical figure: they seem to be bound in a peculiar kind of moral economy in which weakness is strength and vice versa, in which one's strength is the other's innocence and one's weakness the other's guilt. It is in this light that we venture to offer a tentative reading of the enigmatic conclusion: "I obtained the remaining books, but my friend Hawley repeats that Major and Mrs. Monarch did me permanent harm, got me into false ways. If it be true I'm content to have paid the price—for the memory." The Monarchs' worst act of aggression as well as a most precious memory turns out to be their show of utter helplessness; it must be paid for with some "permanent harm," verbally or otherwise inflicted or self-inflicted.

With the difference that the Monarchs' power is entirely illusory we have here a relation of authority such as Barthes describes in his book *On Racine*: "A is not only powerful and B weak. A is guilty, B innocent. But since it is intolerable that power should be guilty, B takes A's transgression on himself. . . . B's acknowledgement is not a generous oblation: it is the terror of opening his eyes and seeing the guilty Father." A note at the bottom of the page aptly names this type of relation: "In contrast to the famous Oedipus complex, we might call this movement the *Noah complex*: one son laughs at the father's nakedness, the others look away and conceal it." The laughing son—the filial aggressor in the Oedipus—is Hawley. His *raison d'être*, besides projecting the narrator's repressed anti-Monarchist aggression ("Ce sont des gens qu'il faut mettre à la porte"), is to confirm and objectify the damage done to him.

This injury may at bottom be the same as that which Geoffrey Hartman writes about when he characterizes the Jamesian consciousness as "the place at which being reveals itself as wounded"; but we do not share his implicit concern for the welfare of being (and other related notions, such as self, consciousness, reality, etc.): nor do we consider that much is gained over Poulet's view, which Hartman criticizes, by saying that "the difficulty is one of being rather than of representation." The particular nature of the wound, according to our diagnosis, is that being itself is already a representation.

This assertion is, of course, paradoxical, since in Western philosophy "being" is something quite different from "representation." No one has labored more patiently and skillfully in recent years to deconstruct this as well as the other polarities which form the system of Western philosophy than Jacques Derrida. In a note to "La Double Séance" he describes the peculiar logic of *mimesis* as it emerges from the Platonic dialogues (a text of no mean importance in the history of being as well). This logic is inexorable: whether resembling it rigorously or not, the imitator (artist, art object, text) is condemned to remain always inferior to the imitated (God, Reality, Truth). But the criterion of resemblance is most obvious in making the model the exclusive source of all value. This is precisely what the Monarchs do when they boast of the resemblance of the drawings made after them. This claim is of course not disinterested, since they themselves are the imitated model: *mimesis* is an ideology, or made to function like one in "The Real Thing." But what if the Monarchs themselves are imitators, if the real thing is itself already a representation? In order to produce art, the artist must master life, that is to say, defuse the paralyzing spell of existing forms by discrediting their claim to ontological (or any other) authority. This is the point of articulation where our two initial polarities form one system, for in the structure of *mimesis* life is to art what master is to slave. It is not enough to reverse this hierarchy: the polarity itself must be inscribed in a text which would unhinge and displace it, perhaps towards a notion of *production* (which is not the binary opposite of *re*-production, since it lays no claim to originality).

This is, however, easier said than done. Once under the spell one forgets that it is only a spell; the danger of being devoured by a paper tiger may be, despite appearances, a real danger. This spectral prestige of forms known to lack the force to which they might have corresponded once has not yet been explained. Clues are to be sought not in truth or untruth of the sign "Major and Mrs. Monarch" in the action, but in its coded meaning in the text. As a literary sign the Monarchs function in a peculiar way: they represent the ruling class, the social order, inherited forms, *authority* in the most abstract and general sense; but at the same time they stand for the ideological gap, the non-adequation of appearance and reality, the arbitrary link between sign and meaning. Authority—one of the meanings of this complex sign—is thus simultaneously constituted and undermined by the other. It can only be demystified in the process of its remystification. If by arguing a certain number of points in a certain order and in print this paper has arrogated to itself some authority, it is hoped that it nevertheless does betray some of its profound inauthenticity.

"The Figure in the Carpet"

J. Hillis Miller

Images of filaments, *ficelles*, lines, figures drawn with lines, woven or embroidered cloth, thread themselves through the dense metaphorical texture of Henry James's prefaces. These prefaces taken together no doubt form the most important treatise on the novel in English. A passage in the preface to *Roderick Hudson* is an appropriate place to begin, since it bears not only on the difficulty of beginning but on the even greater difficulty of stopping once one has begun. In the passage I cite, the issue is a double one: first, how, in writing a novel, to draw a line around the material to be treated, to give it an edge or border which appears as a natural stopping place in all directions beyond which there is nothing relevant to the subject, and, second, how, within those limits, to treat what is left inside the charmed circle totally and with total continuity, omitting nothing and establishing or articulating all the connections, all of what Tolstoy, in a splendid phrase, called "the labyrinth of linkages." Continuity and completeness, on the one hand, and finite form, on the other, this is the double necessity:

> Yet it must even then have begun for me too, the ache of fear, that was to become so familiar, of being unduly tempted and led on by "developments"; which is but the desperate discipline of the question involved in them. They are of the very essence of the novelist's process, and it is by their aid, fundamentally, that his idea takes form and lives; but they impose on him, through the principle of continuity that rides them, a proportionate

From *Poetics Today* 1, no. 3 (Spring 1980). © 1980 by *Poetics Today*, The Porter Institute for Poetics and Semiotics.

anxiety. They are the very condition of interest, which languishes and drops without them; the painter's subject consisting ever, obviously, of the related state, to each other, of certain figures and things. To exhibit these relations, once they have all been recognized, is to "treat" his idea, which involves neglecting none of those that directly minister to interest; the degree of that directness remaining meanwhile a matter of highly difficult appreciation, and one on which the felicity of form and composition, as a part of the total effect, mercilessly rests. Up to what point is such and such a development *indispensable* to the interest? What is the point beyond which it ceases to be rigorously so? Where, for the complete expression of one's subject, does a particular relation stop—giving way to some other not concerned in that expression?

Completeness; continuity; finite form—James here gives masterly expression to this triple necessity in the production of a literary text. Where is the edge of a given subject or relation within that subject? It is obviously a matter of degree, of nuance. What is the difference between "directly" or "rigorously" ministering to interest and only indirectly or loosely doing so, beyond the margin, peripherally? The edge is no sharp boundary but an indefinitely extending gray area, no longer quite so rigorously relevant, but not irrelevant either. At what point does a bit of accrued interest become so small that it can be dispensed with, rounded off to the nearest zero, so to speak? What does James mean here by "figures"? The figures in the carpet? Figures of speech, embroidered flowers of rhetoric? Figures as the persons of the drama? Whatever the answers to these questions, it is clear that for James the necessity of completeness and continuity, reconciled with finite form, can never by any means other than a fictitious appearance be satisfied. The triple necessity is a triple bind.

The reasons for this are multiple. On the one hand, there is in fact no intrinsic limit to a given subject. To represent it completely would be to retrace an infinite web of relevant relations extending to the horizon and beyond, in every direction: "Really, universally, relations stop nowhere." It would appear, however, that this problem could be solved by the arbitrary drawing of a boundary line establishing an edge beyond which the writer will not allow himself to go. The fundamental act of form-giving is the establishment of a periphery. This periphery must be made to appear to be an absolutely opaque wall beyond which there is nothing, or not even a perceptible wall, but an invisible enclosure or reduction, like a piece of music in which the note C cannot appear, or like the limits, no limits, of universe which is finite but unbounded. In such a universe, one can go anywhere, in any direction, but one remains enclosed, without ever encountering walls or boundaries. If "relations stop nowhere," "the exquisite problem of the artist is eternally but to draw, by a geometry of his own, the circle within which they shall happily *appear* to do so."

Even when this reduction of the infinite to the finite has been accomplished, however, the problem of the limitless reforms itself within the magic circle. Continuity is everything for the novelist. This means that every possible relation must be retraced within the circle, every figure drawn on its surface. Since each entity, "figure," or "thing," for James, exists *as* its relations, to represent the figure or thing completely is to represent all its relations. The figure, by a cunning equivocation, is the figure made by the lines which may be drawn between it and other things, other figures. The multiplicity of these lines would be paralyzing if the writer consulted it directly. He has to know it and not to know it in order to focus on one relation without being distracted by all the others. Here is another way in which the narrative line may be described as spun out of its own impossibility. Even the tiniest temporal or spatial gap in the universal continuity would be a disaster. The writer has to be both aware of this necessity and force himself fiercely to ignore it. This is as impossible a task as being told *not* to think of something without being given a positive substitute: "Don't think of your own name." The artist, says James, "is in the perpetual predicament that the continuity of things is the whole matter, for him, of comedy and tragedy; that this continuity is never, by the space of an instant or an inch, broken, and that, to do anything at all, he has at once intensely to consult and intensely to ignore it."

The infinity and hence impossibility of the narrator's task reforms itself, then, within the arbitrarily closed line which was drawn to make the infinite finite. One way to see this infinity of the finite is to recognize an equivocation in the concept of representation, an equivocation also to be encountered in the term *diegesis*. A *diegesis* is the following through of a line already there. A representation is a presenting again of something once present. Any telling is a retelling, a new line different from the first line. Therefore it contains within itself the potentiality of further repetition. One doubling invites endless redoublings.

In the passage which follows the one just quoted, James speaks of life as a featureless canvas. The novelist's work is the embroidery of figures on this surface. Life itself is a woven texture, but an undifferentiated or unfigured one. It contains the possibility of many figures rather than being a single unequivocal figure already present. Representation is the choice of one line to follow with the new thread interlaced from hole to hole on the already woven canvas of life. This new thread makes a figure, a flower on that ground. The same canvas contains the possibility, however, of an infinite number of slightly different variations on the "original" flower, set side by side on the canvas like the figures on a quilt, but intrinsically present as possibilities of the original finite square or circle. They are in fact not only possibilities but necessities. The initial requirement was for total completeness in the retracing of all possible relations.

Here the figure of the embroidered canvas breaks down, like all such figures, and, in its breaking down, as in all such cases, reveals an impasse which was implicit as much as a conceptual as a figurative possibility in the "original" idea to be expressed. The narrative line, word following word, episode following episode, in a linear sequence, makes a configuration, but the latent possibilities of relation in the elements of the presupposed subject demand an indefinite number of repetitive variations on any embroidered figure which happens to come first. These in fact must be thought of as superimposed or simultaneous, with no intrinsic priorities of originality and repetition, though in words they must make a line. In the spatial figure of embroidered canvas they must falsely be imaged as separate flowers side by side, extending outward in every direction on a canvas which, at first a figure for the finite surface enclosed within the charmed circle the artist has drawn by that "geometry of his own," now must become "boundless" once more, since it is the paradoxical unfolding of the infinity implicit in the finite. All the flowers possible on a single circle of canvas cannot be imaged in that circle but only thought of as an infinitely repeating pattern, each figure somewhat different from the last. "All of which," says James of his claim that the demand for absolute continuity must be both intensely consulted and intensely ignored,

> will perhaps pass but for a supersubtle way of pointing the plain moral that a young embroiderer of the canvas of life soon began to work in terror, fairly, of the vast expanse of that surface, of the boundless number of its distinct perforations for the needle, and of the tendency inherent in his many-colored flowers and figures to cover and consume as many as possible of the little holes. The development of the flower, of the figure, involved thus an immense counting of holes and a careful selection among them. That would have been, it seemed to him, a brave enough process, were it not the very nature of the holes so to invite, to

solicit, to persuade, to practise positively a thousand lures and deceits.

The finite has here become magically infinite once more, according to the paradoxical law, which governs all James's fiction, whereby the more apparently narrow, restricted, and exclusive the focus, as for example on the relations of just four persons in *The Golden Bowl*, the more the novel is likely to extend itself to greater and greater length and even then to be unfinished in the sense of being disproportionate. Each work has what James called a "misplaced middle," a lopsided shape seeking to be hidden by consummate dissimulation, so that the incomplete treatment of certain relations will not appear.

These "flowers and figures," what are they? Is it a question of a single all-inclusive design encompassing the totality of the story, or is it a question of a repeating figure specified and then varied throughout the story? The figure of the flower is an ancient one for figure itself, that is, for "flowers of rhetoric," for the anthology or bouquet of tropes in their use as the indispensable means of expressing by displacement what cannot be expressed properly, in literal language. Of what are James's flowers the figurative expressions? What is the literal for these figures? The answers to these questions are impossible to give. It is a matter of both/and and at the same time of the logical impossibility of having both/and, of having something which is A and not A at once. James's figure is at once single and multiple. It is the figure of the whole and at the same time the figure of the repeated configuration of the detail. Figure is at once a name for the actual "figures" or characters of the story, and at the same time it is the name for relation, for a design which emerges only from the retracing of "the related state, to each other, of certain figures and things."

"Flower" or "figure"—the figure as flower—is James's metaphor for the configuration made by the "realistically" treated human characters and relationships, with all their abundance of psychological and social detail. The realistic human story is the literal of which James's figure of the flower is the metaphor. On the other hand, the characters in their relationships are not the end of the story. They are themselves, in all their referential specificity, the material with which James creates the flowers or figures, the overall design of his story, like a repeated figure in a carpet. The human story is the metaphor of the figure, which, paradoxically, is the literal object of the story, though it is a literal which could never be described or named literally. It exists only in figure, as figure or flower, that is, as catachresis. Catachresis is the rhetorical name for the flower no flower which poisons the anthology of tropes, the odd man out. Catachresis is the name for that procedure whereby James uses all the realistic detail of his procedure as a novelist to name in figure, by a violent, forced, and abusive transfer, something else for which there is no literal name and therefore, within the convention of referentiality which the story as a realistic novel accepts, no existence. This something else is figure, design, the embroidered flower itself.

"The Figure in the Carpet" is James's most explicit allegorical narrative of this procedure, but it is of course the procedure of all his fiction, and in fact of fiction in general. It is not self-referentiality which subverts the assumptions and procedures of realistic fiction, since self-reference is still reference and therefore is assimilable into the assumptions of mimetic representation. This means that all those Anglo-American studies of the novel which trace the supposed gradual development within it or constant presence within it since Cervantes of self-reflection on its own procedures remain, in spite of their considerable sophistication, caught in the false assumptions of mimetic representationalism. Examples of such books are Robert Alter, 1975, Peter Garrett, 1969, Alan Friedman, 1967, and Frank Kermode, 1968. Self-referentiality is the mirror image of extra-referentiality. The former imperturbably reaffirms the assumption of the latter, since the notion of self-reference depends for its definition on the assumption that there could be such a thing as a straightforwardly realistic novel, from which the self-referential novel is a deviation, modification, or development. The more or less hidden presence of catachresis in one way or another in any "realistic" narrative, for example in the fact that there is no "literal" language for the representation of states of consciousness and interior experience, does, however, constantly subvert the claims of literal reference of any realistic narrative, even the claims of straightforward mirroring made by the most apparently simple stories. This subversion makes all realistic narrative "unreadable," undecidable, irreducible to any single unequivocal interpretation.

"The Figure in the Carpet" is a story which mimes this unreadability, on the thematic level, on the figurative level, and on the overall level of its organization as text. As Shlomith Rimmon has argued (1977), "The Figure in the Carpet" is fundamentally uncertain in meaning. It presents clues or narrative details supporting two incompatible readings. Therefore all those critics who have presented "monological" readings of it have fallen into a trap set not so much by the story itself, in its presentation of an enigma which invites definitive clarification, as by their false presupposition that each work of literature has a single, logically unified meaning. Rimmon's definition of ambiguity, however, is too rational, too "canny," too much an attempt to reduce the *mise en abyme* of any literary work, for example the novels and stories of James, to a logical scheme. The multiple ambiguous readings of James's fictions are not merely alternative possibilities. They are intertwined with one another in a system of unreadability, each possibility generating the others in an unstilled oscillation. Rimmon's concept of ambiguity, in spite of its linguistic sophistication, is a misleadingly logical schematization of the alogical in literature, that uncanny blind alley of unreadability encountered ultimately in the interpretation of any work.

The notion of unreadability must be distinguished, in one direction, from a definition of ambiguity in literature as plurisignificance or richness of meaning. In the other direction, the notion of unreadability must be distinguished from that perspectivism which holds that each reader bring something different to a text and so the text has a different meaning for each reader. Though the insight into ambiguity and irony in the New Critics, for example in Empson (from which, by the way, Rimmon distinguishes her concept of ambiguity), goes beyond the notion of plurisignificance, nevertheless, such insights tend to be covered over or controlled, within the New Criticism, by the notion of organic unity, the notion that a work has total and totalizable significance, even if that totalizing is an insight which the critic can never satisfactorily express in words. Though a literary text is seen as having a richness of meaning which is beyond paraphrase, nevertheless, for the New Criticism, that meaning makes a whole. "Unreadability," on the other hand, is something intrinsic to the words of a work, an effect of the rhetoric or of the play of figure, concept, and narrative in the work, an effect the words of the work impose on the reader, not a result of "reader response." Moreover, instead of rich plurisignificance, the notion of "unreadability" names the presence in a text of two or more incompatible or contradictory meanings which imply one another or are intertwined with one another, but which may by no means be felt or named as a unified totality. "Unreadability" names the discomfort of this perpetual lack of closure, like a Möbius strip which has two sides, but only one side, yet two sides still, interminably.

There is nothing new about the experience of the working of language in literature to which the name "unreadability" is sometimes today given. The great writers themselves through all the centuries of our tradition have tended to know this experience, as their works show. Readers, however, sometimes even writers in their readings of their own work, have tended to be beguiled by the lure of single and totalizable meaning, which is the lure of metaphysics as such. They have tended to believe in the presence of some *logos*, some single meaning for each work. This lure is always present as the other side of the coin of unreadability. Unreadability is the generation by the text itself of a desire for the possession of the *logos*, while at the same time the text itself frustrates this desire, in a torsion of undecidability which is intrinsic to language. The text itself leads the reader to believe that he ought to be able to say what it means, while at the same time making that saying impossible. This, I am arguing, is what "The Figure in the Carpet" is about, though to claim that one can, in so many words, say what it is "about" is of course to succumb to the lure, to take the bait. It might be better to say that the story dramatizes the experience of unreadability, or, rather, since this experience can only be named in figure, it presents figures for it, not least in the recurrent pattern of interpersonal relations which forms the human base for the story's allegorizing of its own unreadability.

The "figure in the carpet" is, on the "literal" level, the figure used by the narrator to formulate his understanding of Vereker's claim that all his work as a novelist is unified by the presence of a single all-inclusive design or meaning which none of his critics has noticed, though it is what all the work is written to reveal. The reader of this admirably comic story must therefore figure out what is meant by this figure in the carpet, and figure out also what is meant by the adjacent terms and figures for this figure which the narrator or Vereker, at one time or another, use:

> "Isn't there," [asks Vereker in his midnight confidence to the narrator,] "for every writer a particular thing of that sort, the thing that most makes him apply himself, the thing without the effort to achieve which he wouldn't write at all, the very passion of his passion, the part of the business in which, for him, the flame of art burns most intensely? Well, it's that! . . .
> . . . there's an idea in my work without which I wouldn't have given a straw for the whole job. It's the finest fullest intention of the lot, and the application of it has been, I think, a triumph of patience, of ingenuity. I ought to leave that to somebody else to say; but that nobody does say it is precisely what we're talking about. It stretches, this little trick of mine, from book to book, and everything else, comparatively, plays over the surface of it. The order, the form, the texture of my books will perhaps someday constitute for the initiated a complete representation of it. So it's naturally the thing for the critic to

look for. It strikes me . . . even as the thing for the critic to find."

The unifying design is here spoken of as an "idea" behind, or below, the work and yet "in" it too. It existed first as a patronizing matrix in the mind of its author, father and mother at once, a generative "passion" or "intention," which was then "applied." What, however, was the base of this idea in the mind of the novelist? "I wondered as I walked away," says the narrator, exasperated at their second meeting by Vereker's refusal to give him any clue to the figure in the carpet of his works, "where he had got *his* tip." After the "idea" has been "applied," the intention fulfilled, it exists as an immanent and yet transcendent pattern within and behind the work, present both in the part of it and in the whole, and at the same time above and beyond the work as its presiding paternal genius. The work as a totality, its "surface," or "texture," or "form," that is, what is superficially visible in it, is a gradually self-completing picture of the figure. The structure in question, one can see, is the basic metaphysical one of the *logos*, of God, for example, as the creative word who is present in all his creations as their ground, as the signature written everywhere in the creation, but who is always present in veiled form, since he can manifest himself, by definition, only in disguised, delegated, or represented appearances. The figure in the carpet is visible, the overall pattern of Vereker's work which ought to stare any critic in the face. At the same time it is necessarily hidden, since anything visible is not it but the sign, signature, or trace of an "it" which is always absent. In short, the figure is precisely a figure, a substitution.

The various figures for this figure, glyphs or hieroglyphs, are dispersed everywhere in "The Figure in the Carpet," whether in local verbal clues, or in the design of interpersonal relations the story makes. All these figures reinforce or restate the traditional metaphysical paradox of the creative *logos*, as well as its always present subversive anaglyph, the "idea" that there is no idea, the idea that the figure behind the surface is a phantasm generated by the play of superficial and visible figurative elements. Neither of these ideas is possible without the other. Each generates the other in a regular rhythm of unreadability, figure and ground reversing constantly.

The development of the story in "The Figure in the Carpet" is punctuated by a wonderfully comic series of clues playing on the various contradictory possibilities latent in the "logocentric" image: that it is within, as contained within container, that it is beneath, that it is behind, that it is a pervasive hidden thread, that it is all surface and no depth and so a fraud, that it does not exist at all, that it is the abyss, that it is a fatal lure, the appearance of food or of satisfaction which destroys the one who yields to its promise. These clues are always figures, since the "it" can only be expressed in figure. There are no literal terms for the "it," which means that these figures are, once more, examples of the figure that explodes the distinction between literal and figurative: catachresis. Rhythm, ratio, or proportion, measure of all—the figure is an idea, a design, a general and organizing intention; subjective as latent theoretical possibility, and yet existing only as objective theatrical pattern; within, behind, below; hidden, and yet revealed; ground, groundless abyss, and yet surface pattern, all three; secret, perhaps phantasmal, thread, and yet the figure made by the visible beads strung on that thread—in short, *logos*.

"Is it a kind of esoteric message?" asks the delightfully obtuse narrator. To which Vereker replies, "Ha my dear fellow, it can't be described in cheap journalese!" Vereker refuses to give any of his readers a clue to his labyrinth because, as he says, "my whole lucid effort gives him the clue — every page and line and letter. The thing's as concrete there as a bird in a cage, a bait on a hook, a piece of cheese in a mousetrap. It's stuck into every volume as your foot is stuck into your shoe. It governs every line, it chooses every word, it dots every i, it places every comma." Immanent law which governs every detail and is therefore present in that detail, as contained within container, foot in shoe, this "thing" has the power of punctuating the line of the narrative, establishing the rhythm of pauses in the chain of signs which is essential to its meaning. It also gives heads to what might otherwise be decapitated, without a ruling energy of capitalization. It dots every i. It gives a ruling law to the miniscule detail by establishing a pervasive law or figure of the whole. At the same time, the "thing" leads the one who sees it by the false promise of satisfaction, of filling, a saturating of emptiness and blandness. This promise, however, leads to a diabolical satire of fulfillment. It leads in fact to the abyss of death. The beautiful caged bird changes in mid-chain of figures into the bait to trap the presumably safely theoretical spectator, watching at a distance, as in a theater. "It" is a food which becomes a means of execution. Vereker's images are as much a warning as a promise. "Give it up—give it up!" he mockingly but also "earnestly" and "anxiously" says to the narrator at the end of their midnight dialogue.

The "general intention" of Vereker's work is, as the narrator guesses, "a sort of buried treasure," visible, audible, or detectable as a faint odor, as "whiffs and hints, . . . faint wandering notes of a hidden music." It is a veiled idol or goddess, and yet visible as a mode of behavior betraying the goddess in her mortal incarnation. This mode is the rhythm of movement in the text itself: *vera incessu patuit dea!* "It's the very string," says Vereker, "that my pearls are strung on!" In short, as the narrator guesses, it is "something like a complex figure in a Persian carpet." Inside, outside; visible, hidden, "It" is also absent, hollow, a hoax, a vacancy: "The buried treasure was a bad joke, the general intention a monstrous *pose*," says the narrator, in exasperation, and later: "I know what to think then. It's nothing!"

The best, and most comic, expression for this last possibility is a significantly displaced one. It is shifted from the work of the strongly masculine, even male chauvinist, Vereker ("A woman will never find out," he says of his secret figure), to the parody of that work in the first novel by Gwendolen Erme, the lady in the story who is fascinated by Vereker's work and who is passed from man to man among the critics who are fascinated by it in their turn. "I got hold of 'Deep Down' again," says the narrator, of her first novel; "it was a desert in which she had lost herself, but in which too she had dug a wonderful hole in the sand—a cavity." The title and the figurative description of this novel, the title of Gwendolen Erme's second, slightly better, novel, *Overmastered*[!] ("As a tissue tolerably intricate it was a carpet with a figure of its own; but the figure was not the figure I was looking for"), the title of Vereker's last work, *The Right of Way*, and the name of the journal for which the narrator, Corvick, and the others write reviews, *The Middle*—all these are dispersed clues, the names of absent and unattainable texts. These titles reinforce the image of a journey of penetration, crossing barriers, reaching depths, but remaining always, precisely, in the middle, on the way. With however much of a right of way one is never finally in the arcanum. One remains always face to face with some mediating sign, obstacle as well as promise, trace of an absence.

This structure is repeated in the chain of interpersonal relations which organizes James's story. It is a chain so absurd, when the reader thinks of it, as to be one of the major sources of comedy in the tale, what the narrator calls "a series of phenomena so strangely interlaced." Behind the whole series is Vereker's sick wife. Her illness, "which has long kept her in retirement," is the reason the great novelist goes south, never to be seen again by the narrator. His friend, Corvick, however, identifies the figure in the carpet of Vereker's work in a flash of intuition. Corvick visits Vereker in the south to have his insight confirmed. Presumably he passes his secret on to his wife Gwendolen (or does he?). She in turn may or may not have given her secret to her second husband, the egregious Drayton Deane, though Deane appears to be honest in his denials of knowledge. One by one, after Vereker's death, and then after the death of his wife (who probably, the narrator says, had never seen the figure in the carpet anyway), the possessors of the secret die. They die so abruptly and so fortuitously as to suggest that possession of this secret is deadly, like looking on the goddess naked. The newly-married Corvick falls from a dogcart on his head and is killed on the spot, leaving his critical essay on Vereker, which was to have revealed all, a mere useless fragment. Gwendolen, who has married Corvick and presumably received the secret as a wedding present, then marries Drayton Deane, but dies in childbirth without telling the narrator the secret and perhaps without having revealed it to her new husband either.

The passing on of the secret obviously has something to do with sexual intimacy and sexual knowledge. The narrator's "impotence" seems connected with his celibacy, though both he and Drayton Deane at the end of the story are left equally "victims of unappeased desire," in spite of the fact that Deane was not celibate. "Corvick," says the narrator, "had kept his information from his young friend till after the removal of the last barrier to their intimacy—then only had he let the cat out of the bag. Was it Gwendolen's idea, taking a hint from him, to liberate this animal only on the basis of the renewal of such a relation? Was the figure in the carpet traceable or describable only for husbands and wives—for lovers supremely united?" What *is* revealed in sexual knowledge? Is it nothing at all? Is sexual experience a figure of death, an absence, the absence of any heading power, any law able to put dots on the i's, or is it rather some ultimate presence, capital source or phallogocentric origin, yarn beam, loom (*istos*), on which is woven the figure in the carpet? Is that figure the figure of nothing, or is it the figure of the *logos*? There is no way to know. James's story remains alogical, caught in the oscillation among these various possibilities. It remains a *mise en abyme* of analogies, not least important of which is the analogy between the frustrated activity of decipherment performed on Vereker's work by the narrator and that performed on James's own figure in the carpet by any reader.

To return, then, after this digression (or is "The Figure in the Carpet" not smack in the middle of the right of way?), to James's preface to *Roderick Hudson*. There the figure of the figure in the carpet is, the reader will remember, both figurative and literal, both a name for the design of relations among the human figures in the story and the "it" which is the literal goal of the story, as the young author works away month after month at his "pale embroidery." The images of cloth and the figures woven on that cloth reappear, in fact, both before and after the passage I began with from the preface, in obedience to the law of that compulsion to repeat which seems intrinsic to signs. It seems as though signs must have a genetic life of their own, like some viral energy of replication appropriating foreign conceptual material to their own shape.

It is by way of the metaphor describing *Roderick Hudson* as his first adventure out of the shallow waters of the short story into deep water in the larger ship of the novel that the metaphor of canvas is first introduced: "The subject of 'Roderick' figures [!] to me vividly this employment of canvas, and I have not forgotten, even after long years, how the blue southern sea seemed to spread immediately before me and the breath of the spice-islands to be already in the breeze." After this figure, introduced so casually and so artificially (in the sense that its figurative nature is made obvious), is fully exploited in the theoretical paragraph I discussed above, it reappears once more in the subsequent return to reminiscences about the writing of *Roderick Hudson*. It returns as an image of the fact that the novel had not been finished when it began to appear in monthly parts. This fact "is one of the silver threads of the recoverable texture of that embarrassed phase." The sequence of paragraphs is like a quilt with squares in repeating patterns.

How can this series of compulsive duplications be stopped from proliferating endlessly? This is the question James addresses at the end of the theoretical development of the image of the embroidered flower. The image is of a seduction. The embroidering novelist, "masculine" perhaps in his activity of piercing all those little holes with his needle, is "feminine" in his act of "covering" them and in the passivity of his yielding to the invitation of the perforated surface. He follows it wherever it may lead. It is, the reader will remember, "the very nature of the holes so to invite, to solicit, to persuade, to practise positively a thousand lures and deceits." The problem, once the writer is led astray, seduced, is how ever to stop. He must initially assume that there is some loving fatherly power, paternal and patronizing. This father would govern the whole and give it visible boundaries, a beginning and an end. Such a power would act as the law or *logos* of the whole fabric.

Alas, no such power exists. The writer must act as his own father, in an act of self-generating which is at the same time a self-mutilation, an act of surrender and sacrifice. The writer can come to an end, make form, preserve himself from the abyss of the interminable, only by his willingness to practice a *découpage* at the moment of "cruel crisis." This crisis is an encounter at the crossroads which reverses the Oedipal murder. The artist as father, as patron, cuts off the potentially infinite power of the artist as son, as weaver, as artificer. Only this act of giving up can draw the line which makes narrative possible, defining narration as a feminine and at the same time masculine activity of embroidery. It pierces the little holes on the prepared canvas with a threaded needle and makes the figure in the carpet:

> The prime effect of so sustained a system, so prepared a surface, is to lead on and on; while the fascination of following resides, by the same token, in the presumability *somewhere* of a convenient, of a visibly-appointed stopping-place. Art would be easy indeed if, by a fond power disposed to "patronise" it, such conveniences, such simplifications, had been provided. We have, as the case stands, to invent and establish them, to arrive at them by a difficult, dire process of selection and comparison, of surrender and sacrifice. The very meaning of expertness is acquired courage to brace one's self for the cruel crisis from the moment one sees it grimly loom.

A Jamesian About-Face:
Notes on "The Jolly Corner"

Deborah Esch

> *And we know how the possible — that ghostly and unreal life of what might have been, figures with which we have a standing rendezvous — exerted a dangerous, sometimes almost insane attraction on James, which perhaps art alone enabled him to explore and exorcise.*
>
> MAURICE BLANCHOT

The question of unrealized possibilities—of what one might have done, who one might have become, had circumstances been different—is posed with notable persistence in James's narratives, the autobiographical and critical as well as the fictive. ["Unrealized," according to *Webster's Third New International Dictionary*, also denotes "not turned into cash by sale," as the house on the jolly corner is not, as well as "not recognized or known," as the *alter ego* is not. Harry Levin's claim that "It is the business of fiction to explore what might have been, what may be, and what is not" implicitly acknowledges the several aspects of "unrealized." His view of "The Jolly Corner" as a "diagram" of the relationship between writer and character is a suggestive one (see *The Power of Blackness* [New York: Random House, 1958]).] Dencombe, the figure for the writer in a tale called "The Middle Years," is a dying novelist obsessed with the idea of revision (the reader finds him compulsively correcting the proofs of what turns out to be his last novel, *The Middle Years*), with the books he might have written and might still write if he could only get, as he laments, an "extension." When a number of prominent authors were asked, during a recent symposium on

---

From *ELH* 50, no. 3 (Fall 1983). © 1983 by the Johns Hopkins University Press. © 1985 by Deborah Esch.

literary composition, to reflect back on their own careers in order to name the work they would most like to have produced, at least one participant recognized a Jamesian note in the question, and responded in kind:

> In a story by Henry James, "The Jolly Corner," a man at night looks in an empty house for the ghost of the person he could have been if his life had been different. The house is that of his youth. In it, thus, are all the possibilities that have not come true. At dawn the man sees his ghost, and it frightens him. This is the story I would have wanted to write, or that I would have wanted to live, or the story in which I identify myself when I try to imagine the books that I could have written instead of those I have.

With his choice of James's late ghost story, Italo Calvino, himself a raconteur with a penchant for the fantastic, provides a concise plot summary along with an appropriate point of departure for a reading of "The Jolly Corner." Like Spencer Brydon, the tale's protagonist, Calvino is asked to conceive of "possibilities that have not come true" for him, and he finds the question itself thematized in the work he would have written. What is more, Calvino not only identifies the story, but does so several times over, in a process of revision punctuated by "or" that, in effect, opens two distinct avenues of interpretation to other readers of the tale.

On the one hand, the story might be read as "the exploration of a consciousness and the education of a perception"—that is, as a narrative of self-identification ("the one in which I identify myself") and eventual self-consciousness on the part of character (Brydon) and reader (here, Calvino). In this light, altogether familiar in the criticism of James's fiction, "the house on the jolly corner, like the House of Usher, becomes the emblem of a mind," and the tale is understood to enact the painful ordeal of that mind as it struggles to fuller consciousness of itself. On the other hand, a slight shift of emphasis in Calvino's assessment would suggest that "The Jolly Corner" might be read in another light as well: the story he would have wanted to write, the one that comes to mind when he tries to imagine the books he could have written, might be approached in terms of reading (and self-reading) and writing (and self-writing). The many attentive interpreters who have traced and retraced the Jamesian "coming to terms" in the psychological and the epistemological senses of a character's becoming reconciled to his or her hard-won self-consciousness tend to overlook the other, rhetorical significance of the activity of mind indicated by this phrase: namely, that of finding the "terms" that will turn its experience into a writable, readable narrative. It is presumably clear, even to the reader for whom language as such is not an issue in the fiction, that the crucial terms arrived at by the Jamesian consciousness (whether narrator or character) are invariably terms of comparison, or metaphors. Yet this observation is generally relegated by the critics to a discussion of style or technique as categories understood to subsume this aspect of the prose, rather than serving as a spur to the interpretation of the pervasive figures of speech themselves. This neglect of James's consistent and explicit appeal to figurative language is particularly perplexing in the case of "The Jolly Corner," a tale that turns upon the consequences, for character, narrator, and reader, of "strange figures" lurking in the text in the guise of familiar idioms. For the reader who acknowledges the force of these metaphors, the suspense attending this ghost story is displaced from the recounted act or event to the narrative's textual surface. The "ordeal of consciousness," in this exemplary Jamesian narrative, is a function of the process of figuration that it thematizes—of the ordeal, that is, of reading and writing.

"The Jolly Corner" was first published in December 1908 in Ford Madox [Ford] Hueffer's newly founded *English Review*, after suffering rejection by a number of other editors. In keeping with James's characteristic practice of revision, even this late tale underwent minor modification as it passed from the journal to volume 17 of the New York Edition. In most respects, however, the two versions are identical: they recount a critical moment in the history of Spencer Brydon, a middle-aged American expatriate who, after a sojourn of thirty-three years in Europe, returns to New York and his ancestral home. To this extent, the tale has some autobiographical basis, and critics have rightly recognized aspects of the author's career in that of his character. James returned to his birthplace in 1904, following an absence of twenty-two years, on a journey that is documented in the essay "New York Revisited," collected in *The American Scene*. Like Brydon, James finds the city greatly changed, in ways he had not anticipated. He articulates his ambivalence, as a "revisiting spirit," by way of a figure of writing, of inscription: "It was an extraordinary statement on the subject of New York that the space between Fourteenth Street and Washington Square *should* . . . figure as the old ivory of an overscored tablet." The nostalgic narrative of his own history is disrupted by the most drastic alteration James discovers on his homecoming: the "house of his youth" has been razed to make room for "a high, square, impersonal structure" that "so blocks, at the right moment for its own success, the view of the past, that the effect for me, in Washington Place, was of having been amputated of half my history." Having linked the activity of remembering with one of dismembering, he further figures his disenchantment as follows:

> This was the snub, for the complacency of retrospect, that, whereas the inner sense had positively erected there for its private contemplation a commemorative mural tablet, the very wall that should have borne this inscription had been smashed as for demonstration that tablets, in New York, are unthinkable. . . . Where, in fact, is the point of inserting a mural tablet, at any legible height, in a building certain to be destroyed to make room for a sky-scraper?

Spencer Brydon likewise experiences a mixed response of fascination and dismay on his belated return to New York, and borrows James's figure of the "overscored tablet" when he compares the city to "some vast ledger-page, overgrown, fantastic, of ruled and criss-crossed lines and figures." He is repelled by the philistine values everywhere in evidence, judging them "vulgar" and "monstrous" (epithets that will reappear later in the story). But Brydon's perspective is not "blocked," his history is not "amputated," by the unexpected loss of his birthplace sustained by James. He is the possessor of two properties in the city, and has returned in part to inspect them, their rent having financed his life abroad. One of these, the unoccupied house on the site named in the title, is his ancestral home. It is also the house he comes to haunt in pursuit of the character he might have been had he lived those thirty-three years in his native city. Brydon's nightly vigil in the great vacant structure culminates in a stunning scene of recognition, when his *alter ego*, the "I" of his increasingly obsessive "I might have been," finally materializes and confronts him face to face.

Thematically, "The Jolly Corner" broke little new ground for James. Brydon's pilgrimage to New York is in some respects a revision of that of Clement Searle, the protagonist of "The Passionate Pilgrim," a tale written more than thirty years earlier. And the preliminary notes for James's last novel, *The Sense of the Past*, record the use he made of a "scrap" of that unfinished work, which also featured a ghost of sorts, in composing "The Jolly Corner." In the story-line borrowed for the shorter narrative, the

> hero's adventure there takes the form so to speak of his turning the tables, as I think I called it, on a "ghost" or whatever, a visiting or haunting apparition otherwise qualified to appall *him*, and thereby winning a sort of victory, by the appearance, and

the evidence, that this personage or presence was more over-
whelmingly affected by him than he by *it*.

The language in this excerpt from the notebooks rehearses the earlier
account, in the autobiographical volume *A Small Boy and Others*, of a memo-
rable scene of James's childhood—the Galerie d'Apollon in the Louvre, an
old haunt of his youth—and the setting it provided for a dream he had later
in life. The climax of the dream that James called "the most appalling yet
most admirable nightmare" of his life was

> the sudden pursuit, through an open door, along a huge high
> saloon, of a just dimly-descried figure that retreated in terror
> before my rush and dash . . . out of the room I had a moment
> before been desperately, and all the more abjectly, defending by
> the push of my shoulder against hard pressure on the lock and
> bar from the other side. The lucidity, not to say the sublimity,
> of the crisis had consisted of the great thought that I, in my
> appalled state, was probably still more appalling than the awful
> agent, creature, or presence, whatever he was. . . . The triumph
> of my impulse, perceived in a flash as I acted on it by myself at a
> bound, forcing the door outward, was the grand thing, but the
> great point of the whole was the wonder of my final recogni-
> tion. Routed, dismayed, the tables turned on him by my so
> surpassing him for straight aggression and dire intention, my
> visitant was already but a diminished spot in the long perspec-
> tive, the tremendous, glorious hall, as I say, over the far-
> gleaming floor of which . . . he sped for *his* life.

The "final recognition" James alludes to—that he has prevailed over
"the awful agent, creature, or presence"—is predicated on a prior *self*-
recognition on the part of the dreamer; insofar as James is able to identify
himself as the first person in the nightmare, the account can constitute
further autobiographical material for the story he would subsequently
write. In both of the passages cited, the idiomatic expression "turning the
tables" is used to convey the essential affair of the narrative, which in each
case is an act of reversal performed by the protagonist. Spencer Brydon
credits himself with the same fait accompli in the text of "The Jolly
Corner," when he reflects, by way of a rhetorical question, on the turn his
situation has taken: "People enough, first and last, had been in terror of
apparitions, but who had ever before so turned the tables and become
himself, in the apparitional world, an incalculable terror?" "Turning the

tables" is a figure of speech based on a meaning of "table" other than that invoked earlier, of a tablet bearing or intended for inscription, a memorial plaque fixed in a wall, or a notice-board (*OED*); the sense of "table" in James's recurrent phrase is that of a game-board, as in chess. The player who does the turning rotates the board so as to reverse the relative positions of the opponents, putting each in the other's former place. In James's dream and in the story, the protagonist's sense of "victory," of "triumph," consists in his having effected such an about-face. On the night following his third absence from the house, calculated to lull his quarry into a false sense of reprieve, Brydon recommences his vigil with a fresh certainty, formulated in terms of another analogy with a bigger game: "'I've hunted him till he has "turned": that, up there, is what has happened—he's the fanged or the antlered animal brought at last to bay'." The cornered prey, according to the metaphor of the chase, senses that escape is impossible and is obliged to turn and face the hunter.

The "turning" that Brydon attributes to his own cleverness and persistence in keeping pace with his adversary is placed within the quotation marks that appear with remarkable frequency in James's prose—often, but by no means exclusively, around clichés—to indicate that the word or expression quoted signifies in the manner of "so to speak" or "as it were"— that is, figuratively. It is not, then, a literal turning that Brydon is convinced has taken place, but a revolution of another sort. Immediately following his reflection, the narrative first person intrudes, as it will do no more than three times in the course of the tale, to emphasize the decisiveness of Brydon's coming-to-terms: "There came to him, as I say—but determined by an influence beyond my notation!—the acuteness of this certainty." It is an arresting moment in the story, marking an unbidden and seemingly unwarranted confession: it represents, in fact, the intervention of the narrator to call into question the possibility of a sufficient narration. Is the reader, then, to understand this interjection as an expression of undue self-effacement on the part of the narrator, who has so far been equal to the twists and turns of Brydon's obsessive pursuit? If so, it is curious that a second such intrusion is made for the express purpose of affirming the adequacy of the narrative notation to what is transpiring:

> Discretion—he jumped at that; and yet not, verily, at such a pitch, because it saved his nerves or his skin, but because, much more valuably, it saved the situation. When I say he "jumped" at it I feel the consonance of this term with the fact that—at the

end indeed of I know not how long—he did move again, he
crossed straight to the door.

Once again, the quotation marks around "jumped" indicate not only that
the narrator is citing himself in a gesture of linguistic reflection, but also
that he is using the term figuratively, to signify a moment in Brydon's
thought process. In this case, the character's subsequent action, his virtual
leap across the room, justifies the narrator's "notation" by literally acting it
out. In the earlier instance of intrusion, the operation of an "influence
beyond his notation" might, of course, rather be understood as a narrative
strategy in keeping with the ostensibly uncanny, supernatural elements of
the tale. But whether the remark is read ironically or taken at face value, it
remains for the reader to pursue the logic and validity of the claims here
being made, by character as well as narrator. This entails posing interpre-
tive questions that are, once again, rhetorical: not because they are necessarily asked in order to produce an effect rather than to elicit a reply, but
because they can be answered only with respect to the rhetorical structures
and strategies in the story. Has Brydon succeeded, as he here persuades
himself, in "turning the tables" once and for all to vanquish his *alter ego*?
And is there indeed at work in the tale a determining influence that is
beyond the narrative's ability to account for it?

The two questions—of the status of Brydon's relation to the figure
for his other self, and of the status of narrative notation—are, to a considerable extent, congruent. In fact, Brydon sees his life as a linear history,
a time-line along which he can trace actions and events backward and, at a
fork in the path marking two incompatible routes, choose (albeit hypo-
thetically) the alternate one. He longs to rewrite the story of his life from
the moment of that choice, recover his lost opportunities, and rescue his
unfulfilled potential. From the outset, before he is even conscious of its
character and scope, Brydon's obsession with his conditional-imperfect past
is articulated most forcefully by way of his own explicit metaphors and
analogies, notably those already mentioned whose terms involve pursuit
and confrontation. Early in the tale, his companion and confidante Alice
Staverton observes, with the "slightly greater effect of irony" that distinguishes her version of the matter from Brydon's, that in view of the apti-
tude for business he has demonstrated in an exchange with a building firm
representative, he has clearly neglected a real talent, a genius in fact, and
could doubtless have "anticipated the inventor of the sky-scraper" if he had
remained in New York. Her words constitute a refrain ("If he had but

stayed at home. . . . If he had but stayed at home") and strike a chord that reverberates in Brydon's consciousness long after they are spoken, prompting his own speculation:

> It had begun to be present to him after the first fortnight, it had broken out with the oddest abruptness, this particular wanton wonderment: it met him there—and this was the image under which he himself judged the matter, or at least, not a little, thrilled and flushed with it—very much as he might have been met by some strange figure, some unexpected occupant, at a turn of one of the dim passages of an empty house. The quaint analogy quite hauntingly remained with him, when he didn't indeed rather improve it by a still intenser form: that of his opening a door behind which he would have made sure of finding nothing, a door into a room shuttered and void, and yet so coming, with a great suppressed start, on some quite erect confronting presence, something planted in the middle of the place and facing him through the dusk.

As Brydon's analogy unfolds, his conception of what he might have been, which has itself no phenomenal existence, assumes the shape and substance of this "strange figure" as a result of what the narrator terms "the strangest, the most joyous, possibly the next minute almost the proudest, duplication of consciousness." But the vocabulary of consciousness cannot sufficiently account for the structure of Brydon's reflection and the specificity of the form it generates. What escapes the character, and apparently the narrator as well, is the realization that Brydon's agency (which for him, as avowedly for James, consists in his ritually turning the tables to triumph over his *alter ego*) in fact manifests itself as an ongoing activity of literalization, a turning of the tables on his own figures in an effort to fix their significance once and for all. With his nocturnal vigil on the jolly corner, he grants "all the old baffled forsworn possibilities" of the life he has missed precisely the form that a visiting apparition might have:

> What he did therefore by this appeal of his hushed presence was to wake them into such measure of ghostly life as they might still enjoy . . . they had taken the Form he so longed to make them take, the Form he at moments saw himself in the light of fairly hunting on tiptoe . . . from room to room and from storey to storey.

If the criticism of consciousness has no precise name for Brydon's "strange figure," for the "Form" with a capital *F* that he grants his imagined past, rhetoric can supply the missing term: *prosopopoeia* designates the figure that makes present to the senses something abstract and not susceptible of phenomenalization. In giving a face (*prosopon*) or the semblance of one (*prosopeion*, a later variant denoting *mask*) to an entity that lacks a literal visage, prosopopoeia serves as a guarantor of its existence. In its stricter sense, prosopopoeia is usually accompanied by personification, and often by apostrophe (it is the conventional figure of address in lyric poetry, and constitutive of the form of the ode). According to Pierre Fontanier in his rhetorical handbook *Les figures du discours*, prosopopoeia consists in

> somehow staging [*mettre en scène*] the absent, the dead, super-natural beings, or even inanimate objects, to make them act, speak, respond; or at least to take them for confidants, witnesses, guarantors, accusers, avengers, judges; and this, either in jest [*par feint*] or in earnest, depending upon whether one is master of one's imagination.

While his preoccupation is evidently in earnest, whether Spencer Brydon is master of his imagination, and of the images it figures forth, is a pressing question for a reading of "The Jolly Corner." The obsession with his *alter ego* takes on the form, the phenomenality, of the "strange figure" in order to satisfy Brydon's own design; it is thus no longer, to his mind, merely conceptual and so subject to doubt, but can afford him the clarity and distinctness of a perception whose "sense" is perfectly accessible: "He knew what he meant and what he wanted; it was as clear as the figure on a cheque presented in demand for cash. His *alter ego* 'walked'—that was the note of his image of him, while his image of his motive for his own odd pastime was the desire to waylay him and meet him." But Brydon, in his eagerness to confront his other self, gets his figures confused: it seems he cannot tell (or cannot admit) the difference between the figure indicated on a check, a number that represents a fixed amount of money and can be exchanged on demand for that sum, and the "strange figure" of his earlier analogy—the prosopopoeia—to which he is attempting to assign as stable a significance by literalizing it—that is, by turning what he might have turned into an actual, palpable presence. In other words, Brydon cannot read the word "figure," though he uses it repeatedly, because he cannot tell (or admit) the difference between its literal and figurative senses. He has forgotten, if he ever knew, that the figure of his *alter ego* is a figure by virtue of the linguistic process of figuration. Moreover, he is unable to read the quotation marks that are of his own inscription, unable to tell (or admit) the difference between walked and "walked." His claim to knowing "what he meant and what he wanted" becomes a self-deception based on a refusal *not* to literalize his own figures of speech.

This self-mystification sometimes takes the form of delusions of grandeur—Brydon is convinced that no one before him has ever achieved a frame of mind or forged a set of circumstances comparable to his own. He imagines himself, at one point in his adventure, as a Lancelot figure undergoing a test of courage:

> This was before him in truth as a physical image, an image almost worthy of an age of greater romance. That remark indeed glimmered for him only to glow the next instant with a finer light; since what age of romance, after all, could have matched either the state of his mind or, "objectively," as they said, the wonder of his situation? The only difference would have been that, brandishing his dignities over his head as in a parchment scroll, he might then—that is in the heroic time— have proceeded downstairs with a drawn sword in his other grasp.
>
> At present, really, the light he had set down on the mantel would have to figure his sword; which utensil, in the course of a minute, he had taken the requisite number of steps to possess himself of.

In the final sentence in the passage, the narrative voice resumes a description of the action, and reminds the reader that the instrument Brydon brandishes is not "really" the imagined sword; he merely gets hold of the closest figural facsimile, the candle, since there is no literal rapier at hand. But the text affords Brydon numerous other opportunities to practice his penchant for literalizing his own figures of speech. In an exchange with Alice Staverton, he offers an analogy for his "rage of curiosity" about what might have been:

> [It] brings back what I remember to have felt, once or twice, after judging best, for reasons, to burn some important letter unopened. I've been sorry, I've hated it—I've never known what was in the letter. You may say it's a trifle . . . I shouldn't care if you did! . . . and it's only a figure, at any rate, for the way I now feel.

The analogy is based, as the reader discovers, on an act Brydon has performed "once or twice" in the past—a gesture that is of course charged
with symbolic significance (the same decisive measure is enacted by Kate
Croy in a pivotal moment near the conclusion of *The Wings of the Dove*,
when she burns Milly Theale's final letter to Densher before he can open
it). In this instance, Brydon insists on the figurative status of his comparison,
as if for Alice's instruction. Yet in another early dialogue, she catches him,
as it were, in the act. When he takes her to see the house of his youth, he
denies having even the ghost of a reason for holding on to it, rather than
capitalizing on its prime location and sacrificing it for financial gain, as
he has the second, inferior property. Alice replies by asking, elliptically,
whether "the 'ghost' of one doesn't, much rather, serve—?" Her intona-
tional quotation marks themselves serve to indicate that "ghost," in his
phrase "ghost of a reason," is a trope, a catachresis. Brydon masks his
uneasiness at her so taking note of his guilty figure with a literalizing
response that tries to make light of her acuity: "Oh ghosts—of course the
place must swarm with them! I should be ashamed of it if it didn't." The
narrative is then given over to conjecture about Alice's subsequent thoughts:

> Miss Staverton's gaze again lost itself, and things she didn't utter,
> it was clear, came and went in her mind. She might even for the
> minute, off there in the fine room, have imagined some element
> dimly gathering. Simplified like the death-mask of a handsome
> face, it perhaps produced for her just then an effect akin to the
> stir of an expression in the "set" commemorative plaster. Yet
> whatever her impression may have been she produced instead
> a vague platitude. "Well, if it were only furnished and lived
> in—!"

The death mask, the prosopopoeia, produces more than the "stir of an
expression," or "a vague platitude": it furnishes the house with the kind of
haunting apparition Brydon alludes to in an offhand way when he literalizes
the phrase "ghost of a reason." Again, he forgets the rhetorical status of the
figure, and seeks to engage it as an opponent in a battle of wits—in the
text's phrase, a "concentrated conscious *combat*":

> He had tasted of no pleasure so fine as his actual tension, had
> been introduced to no sport that demanded at once the patience
> and the nerve of this stalking of a creature more subtle, yet at
> bay perhaps more formidable, than any beast of the forest. The
> terms, the comparisons, the very practices of the chase positively

came again into play; there were even moments when passages of his occasional experience as a sportsman, stirred memories, from his younger time, of moor and mountain and desert, revived for him—and to the increase of his keenness—by the tremendous force of analogy.

The analogy of the hunt is one that James himself uses, in his preface to *The Golden Bowl* and elsewhere, to represent the pleasure he takes in writing fiction, which he calls "the entertainment of the great game," and an "inordinate intellectual 'sport.'" In Brydon's reliance on the metaphor of the chase, "the terms, the comparisons," that he brings into play are in effect denied the "play" of possible signification that is the mark of figurative language; they are instead positively put into practice, enacted by the character's literalizing compulsion, in order that their meaning may become one—and only one—with his purpose. In the opening paragraph of the tale, when Brydon finds his belated return to his native city attended by one surprise after another, he reasons that this "might be natural when one had so long and so consistently neglected everything, taken pains to give surprise so much margin for play." He discovers soon enough that "margin for play" is precisely what he has not given, what he cannot afford to give:

> The great fact all the while however had been the incalculability; since he *had* supposed himself, from decade to decade, to be allowing, and in the most liberal and intelligent manner, for brilliancy of change. He actually saw that he had allowed for nothing; he missed what he would have been sure of finding, he found what he never would have imagined.

Later, when his *alter ego* is brought at last to bay, in the logical conclusion to the figural chain set in motion by the metaphor of the hunt, Brydon again finds what he never would have imagined—"it proved, of all the conceivable impressions, the one least suited to his book." He realizes, namely, that his prey has "turned," and is now tracking *him* at a distance, keeping him (as Brydon imagines) in sight while he remains blind to his own position vis à vis his adversary. Indeed, as Brydon reflects, "prey" has become, "by so sharp an irony"—that is, by the sharp about-face of the figure, the turn of the trope—"so little the term now to apply."

His conviction that the tables have been turned on him is, as the narrator intercedes to emphasize, "determined by an influence beyond my notation." But it is only when Brydon comes upon the closed door to the fourth-floor room with no alternate access (recalling the door in his original analogy, and in James's twice-told nightmare)—the door he is certain he has left open, in accordance with his policy—that he experiences "the violent shock of having ceased happily to forget." When he must (involuntarily) remember the rhetorical status of the figure, the possibility of another agent's being at work presents itself: "Another agent?—he had been catching, as he felt, a moment back, the very breath of him; but when had he been so close as in this simple, this logical, this completely personal act? It was so logical, that is, that one might have *taken* it for personal . . . and this time, as much as one would, the question of danger loomed." The act and the agency in question are "so logical" that they might be taken for "personal"—and are mistaken for such by Brydon in the form of the prosopopoeia, the figure that gives phenomenality to his speculation and desire, to the point of their being incarnated in the person of his projected *alter ego*.

Brydon expresses earlier in his adventure an appreciation for the *im*personal, which he evokes by opening the shutters of the upper rooms out onto the night. He relishes

> the sense of the hard silver of the autumn stars through the windowpanes, and scarcely less the flare of the street-lamps below, the white electric lustre which it would have taken curtains to keep out. This was human actual social; this was of the world he had lived in, and he was more at his ease certainly for the countenance, coldly general and impersonal, that all the while and in spite of his detachment it seemed to give him.

In his anxiety, Brydon takes comfort in the impersonal "countenance"—in the sense of moral support or encouragement—offered him by the vision of the world outside his private ordeal. Now, however, as "the question of danger looms," what he had taken for personal—the operation of the strange figure in the act of closing the door—proves to be the function of another countenance, one he mistook for personal, but which, as a linguistic phenomenon, is strictly impersonal: namely, the countenance of the prosopopoeia by which he has given a face, a form, a personality, to a conception. The potential danger, however, does not arise from any real threat posed by this "prodigy of a personal presence," odious as it appears to Brydon when it finally presents itself to block his escape from the house. The hazard stems from his conceivable loss of mastery over his discourse — from the possibility that his metaphors are out of his control. The figure refuses to be restricted to the significance assigned it by Brydon, and lets him know as much, by way of a sign: "Shut up there, at bay, defiant, and with the prodigy of the thing palpably proveably *done*; thus giving notice like some stark signboard—under that accession of accent the situation itself had turned, and Brydon at last remarkably made up his mind on what it had turned to."

When it is no longer merely the tables that have turned, but the situation itself, the relative positions of the players in this elaborate game are no longer clear, and neither are the "terms to apply." This includes, to some extent, the terms that have organized the reading thus far: literal and figurative, terms that appear, parenthetically, in the text of the tale. Brydon's fear that, if he returns to check on the door closed by the phantom, he might find it open again, and the figure at large in the house, takes the "awful specific form" of the image of throwing himself out the window. It is a chance he decides not to take, opting instead for "uncertainty"; as he heads for the staircase to make his getaway, the narrative attests that he is scared speechless: "He couldn't have spoken, the tone of his voice would have scared him, and the common conceit or resource of 'whistling in the dark' (whether literally or figuratively) have appeared basely vulgar." The quotation marks and parentheses punctuate a new uncertainty, reflected in the "or" of "literally or figuratively." The presentation of both possibilities might be read as another instance of the narrator's irresolution about what is passing through Brydon's mind: he is doubtful as to whether the character is contemplating producing an actual sound, or simply pretending to ignore the threat—"whistling in the dark" in the metaphoric sense (the same figure appears in "The Beast in the Jungle" as well as in *The Ambassadors*). But whether the narrator is here master of *his* discourse or not, the point is that the text will not, cannot decide the question posed by the "or." The possibility that the figure resists being confined to one signification or the other sheds a light on the nature of this uncertainty, revealing it as hesitancy about the adequacy and the ultimate usefulness of a distinction that begins to blur when the language in which it is presented is susceptible to the very indetermination that the distinction tries to prevent.

In this drama—this pantomime—of facts and figures, "the great fact," to allude once more to the second paragraph of the tale, has been and remains "the incalculability," the indeterminacy of the figure—the force that overwhelms Brydon when, in the story's climactic scene, he encounters his *alter ego* in all its identity and difference. The process of figuration has been thorough; the "ghost, or whatever," is rendered in more concrete sensory detail than any other character, any other figure, in the tale, including Brydon himself:

> Rigid and conscious, spectral yet human, a man of his own substance and stature waited there to measure himself with his power to dismay. This only could it be — this only till he recognized, with his advance, that what made the face dim was a pair of raised hands that covered it and in which, so far from being offered in defiance, it was buried as for dark deprecation.

Every fact of the figure's appearance, from its double eyeglass to its polished shoe, becomes visible, to Brydon's great revulsion:

> That meaning at least, while he gaped, it offered him; for he could but gape at his other self in this other anguish, gape as proof that *he*, standing there for the achieved, the enjoyed, the triumphant life, couldn't be faced in his triumph. Wasn't the proof in the splendid covering hands, strong and completely spread?—so spread and so intentional that, in spite of a special verity that surpassed every other, the fact that one of these hands had lost two fingers, which were reduced to stumps, as if accidentally shot away, the face was effectually guarded and saved.

If James, on finding that his birthplace has been torn down to make room for more progressive structures, characterizes the effect as one of "having been amputated of half my history" in the passage from "New York Revisited," Brydon has a literal amputation on his hands. Though the face seems, initially, to be effectively masked despite the two missing digits, it turns out that it is not "saved" in the end, literally or figuratively. The hands fall away to reveal the monstrous visage, and Brydon is not spared the resulting humiliation:

> the bared identity was too hideous as *his*, and his glare was the passion of his protest. The face, *that* face, Spencer Brydon's?—he searched it still, but looking away from it in dismay and denial, falling straight from his height of sublimity. It was unknown, inconceivable, awful, disconnected from any possibility—! He had been "sold," he inwardly moaned, stalking such game as this: the presence before him was a presence, the horror within him a horror, but the waste of his nights had been only grotesque and the success of his adventure an irony. Such an identity fitted him at *no* point, made its alternative monstrous.

While Calvino can cite "The Jolly Corner" as "the story in which I identify myself when I try to imagine the books I could have written," the tale's protagonist fails to identify himself in the figure he has authored. He finds it disfigured beyond recognition: it is not *his* face, but a hideous mask that fails to fit him, and Brydon denies it, losing face and consciousness. He falls into a dead faint, and it appears that he has given up the ghost.

In the story's epilogue, Brydon awakes after an undertermined lapse of time to see the faces of Mrs. Muldoon and Alice Staverton watching worriedly over him, and finds himself with his head cradled in the latter's lap, stretched out on the black and white squares of the hallway. As he regains consciousness, his nightmare and its aftermath are summed up, not surprisingly, by analogy:

> It had brought him to knowledge, to knowledge —yes, this was
> the beauty of his state; which came to resemble more and more
> that of a man who has gone to sleep on some news of a great
> inheritance, and then, after dreaming it away, after profaning it
> with matters strange to it, has waked up again to serenity of
> certitude and has only to lie and watch it grow.

Though Brydon is quick to identify himself with the dreamer in his analogy, there is a confusion in the last pages between waking and sleeping that calls into question his "serenity of certitude" and the status of the entire preceding episode. For if, when one dreams, one invariably dreams that one is awake, the project of distinguishing between waking and sleeping, sensing and dreaming, seeing and hallucinating, is problematized. In thinking (or perhaps in dreaming) that he has (whether literally or figuratively) "waked up again" to knowledge, Brydon may well be deceiving himself once more, and the pursuit of his *alter ego* may have been, like James's appalling and admirable nightmare, only a dream.

Alice Staverton, on the other hand, seems more capable of discriminating between these questionable states. She informs Brydon that she, too, has seen the strange figure, at the same time that it appeared to him—but seen it, as she has twice before, in a dream. To substantiate her claim, she describes the apparition down to the last grisly detail, and her companion has no choice but to believe her: "Brydon winced—whether for his proved identity or for his lost fingers." But whose identity is in fact proved through Alice's testimony? How can either she or Brydon be certain that their respective figures are identical? Alice explains that when the visitant appeared to her she "knew it for a sign," that she was not, like Brydon, horrified by the "poor thing," but could accept him, not "for his proved identity," but "for the interest of his difference." Miss Staverton, to whom the narrator repeatedly attributes a saving sense of irony, allows the figure what Brydon has consistently denied it: a life, and a story, of its own, independent of his authorship and of any attempt to fix the terms of its interpretation. To this extent she is an example for the reader of the tale, who can now turn the tables on its narrator's insistence upon the determining force of an influence beyond his notation, to counter that what is at issue in "The Jolly Corner" is nothing less than a notation—the narrative's system of written signs—that is beyond Brydon's, or Alice's, or the narrator's, or the reader's influence. Notation, the *alter ego* of no one and nothing, is what has finally to be confronted—that is, to be read. Such an alternative reading has, however, its monstrous aspect, for it forces the reader to face his (or her) inability to identify himself (or herself) in the tale that tells the story of what (s)he could have read, and would have read, if reading had been a possibility.

The "Lost Stuff of Consciousness": The Priority of Futurity and the Deferral of Desire in "The Beast in the Jungle"

Donna Przybylowicz

"The Beast in the Jungle" is in some ways an anomaly in the Jamesian canon, for its preoccupation is not with the past but with the priority of the future and one's potentiality-for-being. In all the works that will be discussed [elsewhere], there is a marked resistance to a consideration of futural possibilities that is manifested in the characters' fear of and flight from innovation and change. Discovering rationalization in the whole doctrine and myth of absolute presence and plenitude of being contained in his ancestor's existence, Ralph Pendrel (in *The Sense of the Past*) attempts to accomplish the conquest of time through an exaltation of the past, the platonic concept of anamnesis, which promises the recapture of lost paradises and ideal utopias and represents the triumph of the individual spirit over temporality. For White-Mason of "Crapy Cornelia," Spencer Brydon of "The Jolly Corner," and Mark Monteith of "A Round of Visits," being is no longer fulfilled by a contemplation of the future but by the reassuring recovery of a bygone era. Yet Spencer Brydon and Ralph Pendrel alike come to recognize, after their confrontation with historical and contemporaneous others, human finitude and a necessary temporality as the proper foundation for the self in the world. However, Marcher in "The Beast in the Jungle" is initially fixated not on an accomplished dead past but on the ontological magnetism of the future. The emptiness of his present and the lack he perceives in his life provoke anticipatory projections that have "nothing" as their object: there appears to be no content to these phantasies.

From *Desire and Repression: The Dialectic of Self and Other in the Late Works of Henry James.* © 1986 by the University of Alabama Press.

The utopian realization of his desires seems impossible for him to imagine concretely and is only vaguely described through its metaphoric embodiment in the signifier of the "beast"—something other, which cannot reveal itself directly, yet demands completion and exegesis in the form of a signified, a meaning. Marcher's dissatisfaction with his current life drives him forward and transforms each contingent present moment into a figure of an ultimate presence: temporality is conceived as the desire of the consciousness to surmount an intrinsic ontological lack and to acquire an ultimate identity through the union of subject and object. Finally, because of the void he perceives in his life due to May's death and his recognition of his own finitude, he turns to the past and the fragments of happiness he can find there. So the quality of the desire to project oneself into either a realm of past or future plenitude is similar and represents the evasion of a genuine confrontation with the present and the potentialities inherent in it.

Paradoxically, although involved in this process of positive anticipation, Marcher's existence is a strangely static one in which nothing much happens. Frightened of living or of making changes in his present, he clings to his egotistic self and "saves" himself for some brilliant and overwhelming future experience. A whole lifetime is presented in some fifty pages, and, although many years pass, the narrative rhythm is slow and repetitious and is rendered through summary and the iterative mode, which convey the senseless waste and futility in waiting for the beast to spring. Most of the action focuses on the unknown future and what it might bring, but speculation is not a large part of the activity that engrosses Marcher and May, for they share a tacit belief that avoids naming the concrete nature of the expectations. The object of desire never materializes, as in the other works discussed; instead, it is compared to a beast waiting to pounce, for Marcher simply refuses to recognize May as an objectification of his unconscious desire for love, which reveals his fear of possessing any sexual identity. Thus, the story depicts the tragedy of human isolation and egotism that results in a life that is unlived and unfulfilled: Marcher's belief in his great destiny, whether ultimately an annihilative event or simply an altering experience, causes him to be insensible to ordinary human emotion and knowledge. He has little interest in anything other than his futural "beast."

Even his continuity with his past is almost negated by his exclusive contemplation of and obsession with what-might-be. When he meets May Bartram at Weatherend after several years of separation, he has a vague and fallacious memory of the place and circumstance of their meeting, while she recalls all the details of their former encounters, particularly his account of his prodigious secret concerning his indescribable but significant fate: "he would doubtless have devoted more time to the odd accident of his lapse of memory if he had not been moved to devote so much to the sweetness, the comfort, as he felt, for the future." Initially filled with hope about his great prospects, he finally experiences an existential, nihilistic despair and dejection that evolve from his realization of his inner emptiness —in that he could not respond emotionally to May—and of his lack of social identity—in that he cannot even be publicly acknowledged as fulfilling the role of husband.

Subsequently, he turns to the past and a reexamination of the happiness it now seems to contain. Thus, the retrospections which at first involve Marcher's attention in a vague, peripheral way become of consuming importance only after May's death when the past invokes a morbid and obsessional response in him, for the revelation that floods his consciousness shows him that his egotism is the specter responsible for his loss of May and for his unlived existence. At the end of the story, he ironically discovers that the great adventure he has been awaiting has already occurred, and he recognizes his failure to respond to May's love when she had offered it to him. This realization finally allows him to live, although in a limited, passive way, for his introduction to death is his initiation into life and his own sense of finitude. The demise of May is felt as the disappearance of a shield protecting him from the fact of his own mortality: "The inauthentic temporality of everyday Dasein [which is 'fleeing *in the face of death*'] . . . must, as such a looking-away from finitude, fail to recognize authentic futurity and therewith temporality in general." Marcher's final conversion to humanity involves an abandonment of his ego's demands. The psychological emptiness, impersonality, and anonymity he experiences after May dies allow him not only to love for the first time but also to accept his role as a complete man. Yet it is all too late: he can no longer contemplate the future with hope; he can only envision his end. What pleasure remains for him consists of re-experiencing the past or imagining hypothetical alternatives to what has occurred, which would offer him the consummation and fulfillment denied to him in reality.

The idea of the unlived life is to be found in many of James's works, but this theme, in combination with others in "The Beast in the Jungle" (i.e., the rejection of the past and the focus on an empty present and an amorphous future), is most markedly manifested in "Fordham Castle." Abel Taker and Mrs. Magaw, alias C. P. Addard and Mrs. Vanderplank, live in "exile" in a European *pensione*: both are "sacrificed," "shelved" by their families, and are "dead" to the world in terms of their real identities. In order to achieve social acceptance and success, Abel Taker's wife and Mrs. Magaw's daughter have abandoned their relatives to a blank and non-descript present and future existence by cutting all ties to their actual past. Taker/Addard must negate his former identity and assume the unobtrusive, bland facade of an other that possesses no actual historical substance, thus causing a discrepancy between inner and outer being. He is constantly concerned that "the upward flutter into fiction" may result in "a straight and possibly dangerous dive into the very depths of truth"; that is, he fears his duplicity may be discovered.

In this story, individuals who exist in the past are dead to all external appearances in the present and in the projected future. Taker/Addard experiences this negation of his previous life as a kind of mortality, which he proceeds to superimpose on the physical world. Even Mrs. Magaw/ Vanderplank's "mathematical hair" reminds him of death, for it is done "in a manner of the old-fashioned 'work,' the weeping willows and mortuary urns represented by the little glazed-over flaxen or auburn or sable or silvered convolutions and tendrils, capillary flowers, that he had admired in the days of his innocence." And the pension's terrace is his "death-chamber." To the outer world he is nonexistent, for his wife has not only dispossessed him of his public persona and societal role but has denied her relationship to him as well by changing her name from Mrs. Sue Taker to the more pretentious Mrs. Sherrington Reeve. Deprived of a place and a function in the Symbolic structure of society and in the Real historical realm, where the individual has a temporal identity, Taker/Addard represents a nonentity. Finally, when Mrs. Magaw/Vanderplank receives a reprieve from her daughter, who has snared a titled dignitary for a husband and can afford to reveal her mother's presence, the alienated hero is denied the company of the only sympathetic individual who knows the secret of his past and, consequently, feels "as abandoned as he had known he should —felt left, in his solitude, to the sense of his extinction. He faced it completely now, and to himself at least could express it without fear of protest. 'Why certainly I'm dead.'" This sense of nullity results from the external world's nonrecognition of his actual identity: the vacuum in which he lives leads to his feeling of numbness and negation. The destruction of one's past and the subsequent confrontation with the void of an unfulfilled present and a future, about which no hopeful extrapolations can be formulated, render an absolute wasteland. Taker/Addard, at the end of the story, remains passively suspended and paralyzed in this purgatory of anonymity, constitutionally unable to react against external forces, represented by his domineering, status-seeking wife, who wishes to deny his presence. The past is a vacuum for Taker/Addard as it is for Marcher; because both are passive men who make no effort to determine their own futures, they ultimately are faced with the deadness and futility of their lives.

For Heidegger, the priority of the future in the formation of the living present reveals the significance of death for man's existence. Since extinction is always imminent, it makes an individual aware of life's finiteness and limitations, enabling him to live as an active person in the present moment. This is necessary in order to give meaning and direction to one's choices, for the impending denial of continuity forces man to exist in the living present, which he structures in terms of a self-projection into an indefinite but finite future. The only temporal perspective that provides for deliberate decision, for self-creation, for action is futural, where one carefully chooses one's possibilities. Such conscious commitment, which recognizes the prospective nature of all intention, is the mark of Heidegger's use of the word "authenticity." Therefore, the only constructive act can relate to the future.

Marcher, however, does not live with this kind of futural thrust and does not experience what Heidegger calls "anticipatory resoluteness," that is, the expectation of a specific event that determines his present aims and desires. Trapped in a time jungle, Marcher's spiritual search for the unnameable can ultimately bring only death. In his acquisition of knowledge there is no true temporal synthesis, for, although he is concerned with prospective possibilities, he does not examine the relevant past in its constitution of the present and remains fixated on the future. Although Heidegger insists on the priority of futurity in defining the meaning and principle of synthesis in any cognitive act ("The primary phenomenon of primordial and authentic temporality is the future"), experiencing, as a time-consuming action, means that an individual's interests and activities are self-structured into the continuing formation of situational presents which bring selected possible future states and pertinent past occurrences into the continuity of his living present. The past for Marcher ceases to have any relevance, nor is it of any help in determining the future, for, although the present offers him options and opportunities for selection, he takes no active part in the establishment of what is to come. Instead, Marcher lives passively in expectation of an impalpable, unknown destiny and expresses neither a desire to direct his own life nor any interest in any genuine futural possibilities, an action which is crucial to his understanding and constitution of any discernible present. Although his perspective is forward looking, it avoids contact with the past and active involvement in the structuring of the future, and it rejects, as well, interaction with the external world of society. Marcher's empirical concepts do not delimit the realm of his prospective experience, for his expectations are not rational in that they do not offer a limited range of behavioral patterns. The future renders a nothingness. The hero's "anxiety," which even initially has no object and is metaphorically and vaguely expressed through the "jungle beast," is at first not focused on questions of time and death; however, with May's demise, he is abruptly confronted with the transitoriness of life and its goals. In recognizing his mutability, he belatedly accepts his role both in the Symbolic network of society and in the Real historical and temporal realm of change, which represents an authentic mode of existence. The beast is metamorphosed from a static image of disembodied, amorphous hope into a dynamic symbol of spiritual and physical decay.

Therefore, although Marcher lives in expectation of some undefined, earth-shattering event, he makes little attempt nor takes decisive action to accomplish anything. There is no selection of preconceived possibilities that project him from the present into the future. Like Gray in *The Ivory Tower* and like Taker/Addard, he passively allows events and people to act upon him: he is the receptive center around which his world revolves, and, unlike the narrator in *The Sacred Fount*, he does not even try to construct an interpretation of what he observes. Because of this inertia, passivity, and inability to make a deliberate choice among various prospects, his being-in-the-world is basically "in-authentic." The prodigious thing that he will experience "isn't anything" he is "to *do*, to achieve in the world, to be distinguished or admired for." It will simply be something that fortuitously happens to him.

Man's temporal syntheses which organize experience always arise from his encounter with life as future oriented, as requiring an involvement with other people and objects surrounding him. Such interaction Marcher cursorily dismisses as only of peripheral importance, for his most valid experiences necessitate a withdrawal into a subjective universe and a preoccupation with phantasies about the future. The actuality he must face every day in his minor government position is mentioned briefly as constituting an unimportant aspect of his life: Marcher has disengaged himself from any sort of confrontation with an environment that he perceives as unsympathetic and hostile, for his true existence involves an Imaginary, intrasubjective realm of self-reflecting desire. With the elimination of the significance of the external societal realm, the only meaningful human contact he has is with May Bartram, but even this connection with outer reality is tenuous, for the relationship is narcissistic. As a mirror image who echoes Marcher's aspirations, she does not live her own life but experiences the world vicariously through him: "she had, as he might say, got inside his condition":

> What it had come to was that he wore a mask painted with the social simper, out of the eye holes of which there looked eyes of an expression not in the least matching the other features. This the stupid world, even after years had never more than half dis-covered. It was only May Bartram who had, and she achieved, by an art indescribable, the feat of at once . . . meeting the eyes from in front and mingling her own vision, as from over his shoulder, with their peep through the apertures.

Reminiscent of the painting in *The Sacred Fount*, the mask here represents Marcher's social facade, the appearance that he normally shows to society, while the eyes express the desires of the obsessed inner self. May empa-thizes so strongly with him that she sees everything from his perspective, mirrors the response he wants the external world to have, and in this way reinforces his fixation on the significance of the "beast." There is an aspect of Marcher which exists in the consciousness of May, and this is what preserves his identity and causes him to continue his hopeful and futural vigil. Her recognition of his great prospects validates his existence and goals: "The very desire of man . . . is constituted under the sign of media-tion; it is desire to make its desire recognized" that is articulated through the dialectic of self and other, of master and slave.

May is not like the inquisitive and meddlesome confidantes of James's earlier works. Instead, she is shy and able to enter imaginatively into his situation, thus becoming a responsive reflector of his desires and a recipient of his confidences. Like the protagonists in "A Round of Visits," "Crapy Cornelia," and "The Jolly Corner," Marcher needs to share his dreams and desires with someone and is quite dependent upon her, but as in the above cases, the woman's needs are completely subordinated to those of the self-centered male. As his alter ego, May does not live her own life but exists vicariously through Marcher's limited experience of the world. Both live a strangely insulated existence, and their contact with society is tangential and restricted. In their conversations, May refuses gratification of her de-sires and accepts the stifling role as the sustainer of Marcher's egotistical dreams. He persistently refuses to recognize her needs and individuality, and in the following passage, which is first rendered from May's limited point of view and then from the narrator's omniscient position, represses any acknowledgment of her love:

> Behaviour had become for her, in the social sense, a false account of herself. There was but one account of her that would have been true all the while, and that she could give, directly, to nobody, least of all to John Marcher. Her whole attitude was a virtual statement, but the perception of that only seemed destined to take its place for him as one of the many things necessarily crowded out of his consciousness.

She fulfills the role of the silent analyst, holding up a mirror to him and hoping to enlighten him as to the nature and truth of the "beast," of his suppressed love and passion that she quietly reflects. Her lucidity contrasts with the haze of self-deception that engulfs him, for her voice functions as an ironic commentary on his belief that he is destined to experience some great adventure:

> He allowed for himself, but she, exactly, allowed still more; partly because, better placed for a sight of the matter, she traced his unhappy perversion through portions of its course into which he could scarce follow it. He knew how he felt, but, besides knowing that, she knew how he *looked* as well.

Thus, May is an embodiment not only of Marcher's conscious demand for a self-reflecting surface that would reinforce his fetishistic pursuit of the "beast" but also of his suppressed and passional need for her. The repetition and deferral of desire, manifested both in May's consistent subjection of her wishes to Marcher's egotistical fancies and in his obsessed and blind megalomania, are constant throughout their lifetime together. The years pass indiscriminately; only a few scenes are rendered, all of which show the same selfish and life-draining impulses on Marcher's part. He refuses to read or decipher the innuendoes, the double meanings in both her words and gestures; all he wants from her is acknowledgment of his egotistical demands.

This inability for May, and especially Marcher, to deal with the ambiguous and ambivalent meaning of sexuality represents a conflict produced by the simultaneous existence of complex and antagonistic energies: the libido and its repression. The double bind suggested by this self-contradiction and division between two opposing forces produces anxiety in the individual about his being-in-the-world. In Marcher, expression of the libido is subverted and negated by psychic repression, which deletes the signification of the sexual and prevents pleasure and fulfillment. Denying the heterogeneity of desire he perceives embodied in May, trying to expel divisive internal energies by reasserting his unwavering belief in his good motives, in his nonsexual interest in her, he excludes her claims on his affections and reaffirms his faith in a homogeneous, self-reflecting universe where he can freely pursue his monomaniacal "beast." Marcher is constantly rationalizing the innocence of their relationship: it is not an affair and thus not "compromising" May's position in society. He completely blinds himself to her love for him and even goes so far as to see himself as "sublimely . . . unselfish" in excluding her from the danger of his "tiger-hunt" by not marrying her:

> His conviction, his apprehension, his obsession, in short, was not a condition he could invite a woman to share. . . . Something or other lay in wait for him, amid the twists and turns of the months and years, like a crouching beast in the jungle. It signified little whether the crouching beast were destined to slay him or to be slain. The definite lesson from that was that a man of feeling didn't cause himself to be accompanied by a lady on a tiger-hunt.

Obviously, May is equipped to share his "vigil" of "silence" day after day, waiting for the beast to pounce, yet he ignores her feelings entirely by fearfully suppressing any suggestions of the sexual and maintaining an ideal, platonic relationship.

In this narcissistic Imaginary situation established between Marcher and May, mortal reality intervenes and terminates his world of phantasies. The pursuit of his "beast" reveals a void, an absence of reality, and proves to be an illusory and futile undertaking, for, although he first sees in it, and in May as well, a reflection of his own desires and hopes, later it mirrors not only her demise but his inevitable death as well, signifying the cessation of his belief in the awe-inspiring, yet terrifying, future event. He identifies so strongly with her as part of himself that he feels "she was dying, and his life would end"; in observing her as she slowly deteriorates, "he ended by watching himself, as if it had been some definite disfigurement of his outer person," thus emphasizing his lack of ego boundary and his propensity to confound inner and outer.

Earlier, the beast symbolizes a vitality of mind and imagination; however, as the past is metamorphosed into "mere barren speculation," it comes to represent lost opportunity and the deferral of desire, for Marcher feels that May's "dying, her death, his consequent solitude — *that* was what he had figured as the beast in the jungle." For May, the metaphoric beast symbolizes the possibility of love, but, eventually realizing that he will never know this experience, she tells him that the beast has pounced and that his not being aware of it is the "strangeness *in* the strangeness." She then turns to death into which the beast is transformed, but he is still blind to his egotistic disregard for her. Ironically, he misinterprets his self-centeredness for genuine concern and feels that "what was still first in his mind was the loss she herself might suffer" if " 'she should have to die before knowing, before seeing' " the nature of the beast: "the possibility was what most made him sorry for her." He fears losing her "because she had, almost of a sudden, begun to strike him as useful," and he sees her as "capable still of helping him," even though "her light might at any instant go out: wherefore he must make the most of it." Seeing her as the repository of knowledge, he asks her if he will suffer, and she replies " 'Never!',", signifying her realization that he will not be particularly touched by her death. Implying that there is still time for him to admit his love, she tells him, " 'The door's open. . . . It's never too late,' " but Marcher, thinking only of his loss of a confidante and not of May's pain and despair, refuses to read her message and obtusely persists in asking her to reveal the meaning of the beast, for "it sprang up sharp to him, and almost to his lips, the fear that she would die without giving him light." In these final scenes between them, she is desperately hoping that he will say he loves her, and she almost reveals her feelings, hoping for some recognition of her needs: she stands near him, "as if still full of the unspoken," and "what he saw in her face was the truth," which she never overtly states and which Marcher completely fails to interpret. He condemns her to an emotionally sterile existence, leaving her despondent and without solace. Like the characters in *The Sacred Fount*, in living off her vitality and love, he has actively exploited May in order to feed his cannibalistic imagination.

Marcher's pursuit of a signified, a meaning, to be found in the knowledge of the other as embodied in the futural beast, representing the fetish-substitute or sublimation of his desire, situates him in the role of patient/analysand, while May, the receptacle of intelligence and comprehension, fulfills unintentionally the structural function of the analyst. In constantly questioning and plaguing her to reveal the "truth" of the beast, he attempts to possess the signified. Such an act, involving the obliteration of the signifier and its vague and affirmative, yet formidable, connotations about the future, would eliminate the heterogeneity and division of meaning. Ironically, this revelation would expose as well the sexually frightening aspects of his desires and thus would destroy the grandiose, yet illusory and amorphous, nature of the phantasies embodied in the beast. Marcher envisions coercing this mysterious knowledge from May as a pleasurable and cognitive accomplishment, for it would symbolize the successful completion of his "hunt" and the discovery of truth and signification, but unconsciously he realizes this disclosure might prove distressing and discomforting, which is why he persistently refuses to read the message of her suppressed love and passion.

Marcher's reiterative entreaty of May is expressive of a metonymic desire, and the aim of his confidante, and analyst, will be to provoke, through her silence and the frustration of any response of gratification to his request for knowledge, his regression from one stage in the formation of the ego to another, from one signifier of demand to another. This process would involve the dispossession of the narcissistic images in which his ego was constituted through identification, through superimposing his own desires on the world and alienating himself in an other, the grossly inflated, yet undelineated, ideals that are initially embodied in the beast, all of which are responsible for the relinquishment of the truth of his inner being. This dialectic should be continued until the object of lack, his own repressed sexuality and the recognition that the ego has been his creation in the Imaginary, is revealed. However, the analytic situation between May and Marcher is ultimately a failure, for it necessitates the actuality of her death to bring about his realization of both his own egocentrism and his creation of a sterile self-mirroring universe.

With the possibility of May's death becoming more real to him, Marcher begins to consider the alternatives that the future will inevitably force upon him and discovers that only one path is open to him—he must confront the imminence of May's end. However, his passivity continues to immobilize him, for he makes no effort to resist or defy fate by trying to save May and himself from an unfulfilled life. He fails, for, unlike May, who has manifested concern and empathy, he never attempts to understand or identify with her feelings. Theirs is a frustrated, neurotic relationship, and the image of May before her death also symbolizes a pathetic, unlived life, the atrophy of body and spirit when affection is not reciprocated. The familiar room in which they had always met reflects the empty and suffocating psychological situation of Marcher and May:

He had been standing by the chimney-piece, fireless and sparsely adorned, a small, perfect old French clock and two morsels of rosy Dresden constituting all its furniture; and her hand grasped the shelf while she kept him waiting, grasped it a little as for support and encouragement.

The fireless chimney-piece points to their lack of passion, the French clock to their wasted lifetime together, and the rosy Dresden figurines to their petrified, static relationship. This bleak description of their physical environment mirrors the whole emotionally starved and repressed atmosphere of the story.

May is depicted as a "sphinx" or "lily," as knowledge and innocence mixed. There is a somber, ominous aura surrounding her death, for her description is suffused with stark images of coldness and whiteness. Looking as if she "might have been powdered with silver," her face appears "almost as white as wax," and her eyes possess a "strange, cold light." Her "faded green scarf," representing the last vestige of her worn vernal love, is juxtaposed to the dazzling, wintry whiteness and deathlike, atrophied aspects of her appearance and behavior. Although May is shown as perpetually virginal and springlike, these qualities have been subverted, for her inclinations and desires have been repressed and have not been allowed to develop and culminate naturally in a meaningful relationship with Marcher. Instead, like a pressed flower, she has been abnormally preserved and her emotions cruelly suffocated under a "clear glass bell":

> She was a sphinx, yet with her white petals and green fronds she might have been a lily too—only an artificial lily, wonderfully imitated and constantly kept, without dust or stain, though not exempt from a slight droop and a complexity of faint creases, under some clear glass bell.

The redemptive, fertile qualities suggested by May's name are not assimilated by Marcher, who, though verging on the spring, as indicated by his name, is unable to abandon his frozen, solipsistic existence. Ironically, he sees the subtlest changes and shadings in her behavior when they apply directly to his own situation, but he fails to interpret her desperate personal message to him. In thinking only of his own plight and inconvenience, he has ignored reality, living only in illusions.

The aestheticization of May culminates in her dehumanization at Marcher's hands. He attempts to make her an adjunct of himself to mirror his own desires, but, as has been seen, he also sees her as the repository of knowledge from which he is barred, thus, on the one hand, perceiving her in the passive position of a slave and, on the other, in the powerful role of a master. In other words, May is either subordinated to his empty, passive, and anticipatory will, or he becomes subservient to what he envisions as her uncanny, superior comprehension of his fate. He refuses to recognize her desire, and she declines to express or impose her own needs on him. The sense of stagnation pervading the whole text reflects Marcher's impotence, inability to act, paralysis in confronting the future, and his absolute lack and abrogation of will.

Marcher's capacity for love is reduced to self-reflection, and, as a piece of art that he creates, rather than an autonomous, external being that he distantly observes, May mirrors his desires. He has transformed her, the object of his repressed affection, into a masturbatory phantasy, into a self-projection of his imagination, thereby denying her individuality and humanity. May not only reflects Marcher's desires, but also represents the ego ideal that can interpret more perfectly than himself the meaning of the beast. Seeing her in this more authoritative and mystical position of a sibyl or "sphinx," as well as an aesthetic image, a lifeless yet preserved flower, he rejects her sexual incarnation in order to retain the idealistic notion of courtly, unconsummated love; for to possess her would involve the destruction of both his own artistic integrity and their aesthetic relationship and would result in the transformation of art into a living object. In his final meetings with her he wants to maintain the ambiguous nature of their situation and sees her as an icon, a symbol, a mysterious, complex "sphinx," an enigmatic piece of art he cannot interpret. Therefore, as the object of lack, as the cause of desire, she is both the powerful mother figure and the asexual, passive lover. As in *The Sacred Fount*, the worship of a work of art that reflects imaginative desire rather than a relationship with a living being is shown to be a deadly, static endeavor rather than a constantly evolving, dynamic pursuit.

Marcher's suppressed libidinal impulses and love for May are transformed into an amorphous energy that is transferred onto the ideal the beast represents. Like May, the beast is an extension of his own ego, a narcissistic image, and serves not only as a displacement of his sexual desires but "as a substitute for some unattained ego ideal." Because of his infatuation with this idealized futural vision, sexual satisfaction is pushed into the background. As the displaced love object, the beast is perceived as "sublime and precious, until at last it gets possession of the entire self-love of the ego." The phantasied object has finally consumed Marcher and his goals and involves a sacrifice of the "true" self. Thus, both the beast and May

become, through the process of transference, objects of Marcher's deformation of reality, projections both of his conscious demands and his disguised, unconscious, and forbidden desires.

As the impenetrable "sphinx" who possesses the knowledge of the
futural beast's nature and as the artificially preserved object of art, May
Bartram's characteristics reflect the oppositions in James's portrayal of
women: his heroes wish to encase the female within the bounds of their
imagination so that she does not become threatening and overwhelming
and remains instead the passive, silent, yet strong, confidante. Whether
weak or domineering, the female figure is always formidable in James,
and his male characters seem constitutionally incapable of living without
her presence. For Taker/Addard in "Fordham Castle," Mrs. Magaw/
Vanderplank "testified unmistakably to the greater energy of women," and
he also perceives himself as incomplete without his wife: "The real reason
was of course that he was nothing without her, whereas she was everything, could be anything in the wide world she liked, without him." In
"The Bench of Desolation," the male character's passivity, fear, and despair
are contrasted to the vengeful, strong, and domineering qualities of the
female, or in "Owen Wingrave" the young hero who wants to be a writer
is tormented by the rigid, destructive will of his betrothed, who tries to
control him by withdrawing her affection when he refuses to accommodate
her demands by making the navy his profession. Calling him a coward, she
causes his desperate, suicidal encounter with an ancestral ghost. In *The
Ambassadors*, a variety of females threaten the hero. Mrs. Newsome, the
absent yet powerful presence that controls Strether's movements and financial situation from across the sea, is like a manipulative, authoritative
mother from whom he finally breaks after his liberating experience in
Europe. Maria Gostrey, like May Bartram, is a more beneficent yet strong
and resourceful woman, whom Strether treats more as an older, more
knowledgeable sibling, for, at the beginning of the book, the narrator notes
that they are mirror images of one another: "each so finely brown and so
sharply spare, each confessing so to dents of surface and aids to sight, to a
disproportionate nose and a head delicately or grossly grizzled, they might
have been brother and sister." However, Mme. de Vionnet represents the
sexual rather than maternal or intellectual element: having qualities of the
flirtatious seductress, she provokes in Strether a sense of guilt and anxiety.
Torn between two powerful forces, one a maternal figure and the other a
distracting temptress, Strether is also divided between the cultures of
America and Europe, one puritanical, admirable for its energy, ingenuity,

and opportunity, and the other sensuous, attractive for its superior aesthetic, cultural, and social ambiance.

In "The Altar of the Dead," there is also a battle for power between the hero, Stransom, and an unnamed authoress. The latter, who is responsible for stealing the former's "altar of the dead," becomes "the priestess of his altar" and uses it for "her own purpose"—that is, to commemorate the death of his old enemy, Acton Hague, who evidently has wronged both Stransom and this woman. When the hero discovers that his temple is dedicated to this scoundrel, he feels she has extinguished his candles and has caused "a dire mutilation of their lives." Curiously, both live more for the dead than for the living, and Stransom prefers this situation: "There were hours at which he almost caught himself wishing that certain of his friends would now die, that he might establish with them in this manner a connection more charming than, as it happened, it was possible to enjoy with them in life." Then they would be locked within his imagination and memory, perhaps more beautifully present than in real life. Like Marcher and May, Stransom and the woman in "The Altar of the Dead" are involved in a fruitless observation and life-denying pursuit of the past. In this way, they fill their empty lives and are unable to recognize and express their love for one another.

In "Maud-Evelyn," the hero displaces his affection from the living to the dead: he prefers to love the ghost of a young girl he never knew rather than marry a flesh-and-blood woman. Maud-Evelyn's parents pretend that she is alive, and Marmaduke proceeds to take part in the whole unbelievable charade, eventually convincing himself that he has married this impalpable creature and has been left a bereaved widower. In his imagination, he has passed through many stages of experience, thereby avoiding all direct confrontation with actuality; past, present, and future are predicated on phantasy. This situation is curiously like that in "Friends of Friends," where the male character also feels strangely drawn to and possessed by the presence of a dead woman. The female narrator of the story, perceiving similarities in her fiancé and her close friend, wishes them to meet. Manifesting complementary personalities, they also have an almost identical hallucinatory experience in common: each has envisioned one parent at the moment of death. Their actual meeting ironically occurs in a ghostly interview after the demise of the narrator's best friend. Subsequently, the fiancé remains fixated on the latter's image, and his betrothed tells him, " 'How *can* you hide it when you're abjectly in love with her, when you're sick almost to death with the joy of what she gives you. . . . You love her as you've *never* loved, and, passion for passion, she gives it straight back! She rules you, she holds you, she has you all!'" After he dies, six years later, the narrator says it was his "response to an irresistible call," to "an unquenchable desire," suggesting the vampiric hold the dead have on the living. It is as if passion can characterize the Jamesian hero's love only if it cannot be consummated. In all these stories, the male's apparent fear of women and sexuality causes him to lead a chaste life that involves no fleshly union.

Revelation of such emotional inadequacy always comes too late for the Jamesian male figure. With May's death, Marcher slowly disengages himself from the supreme fiction he has created, from the construction of his identity and world out of the material of art and the imagination. With this aestheticization of external reality comes a certain nihilistic denial of otherness and a morbid fascination with self-reflexiveness that, with May's demise, culminates in Marcher's realization of his wasted, egotistical existence and in his passage from the Imaginary order of illusory self-mirroring desires to the Symbolic realm of society and its intersubjective demands. The whole process involves his acceptance of man's inevitable extinction that results in the reunification of death with life in the consciousness, which can only be brought about by the obliteration of repression. Mortality confers individuality, independence, and separateness on life, while its suppression produces opposite symptoms, that is, the neurotic, compulsive return of unconscious instincts, the fear of separation from a protective mother figure, and the fixation on a pattern of dependence. Marcher's impossible quest for the object of lack and his refusal of gratification (*jouissance*) because of his dread of death, exemplified in his inability to register the passage of time, make him accept slavery to the "beast" and the Imaginary realm of self-reflections. He recognizes this subservience in his epiphanic realization of his transitoriness:

> He had been struck one day, after an absence exceeding his usual measure, with her suddenly looking much older to him than he had ever thought of her being; then he recognised that the suddenness was all on his side—he had just been suddenly struck. She looked older because inevitably, after so many years, she *was* older, or almost; which was of course true in still greater measure of her companion. . . . His surprises began here; when once they had begun they multiplied. . . . he waked up to the sense of no longer being young.

It is only in feeling himself to be mortal or finite that he can affirm and obtain recognition of his liberty and individuality and can assert himself in the social/cultural realm of the Symbolic, which he tries to do in a limited way after May's death: he despairs at not being able to claim for himself even the role of her husband in the eyes of the world, and, when he visits the cemetery, he desperately attempts to experience grief by identifying with another mourner's sorrow and loss.

Marcher's realization is not sudden but accomplished over a period of time. Gradually acknowledging the finiteness and temporality of life and recognizing death is all that awaits him, he turns from the hopeful contemplation of the future to the immersion in the past and the happy memories it contains. The beast of death brings about "the extinction in his life of the element of suspense." The vitality of mind and imagination, the transformative experience that it earlier presaged is gone, for, as the past turns into "mere barren speculation," the beast comes to represent not only the deferral and repression of desire, his lost opportunity, and the mistake of passively awaiting the future, but also Marcher's alienation from reality, his blindness and egotism, preparing to pounce on and ultimately destroy him: "no breath sounded . . . no evil eye seemed to gleam from a possible lair . . . so absent in short was any question of anything still to come. He was to live entirely with the other question, that of his unidentified past, that of his having to see his fortune impenetrably muffled and masked." The beast and May are symbolic of the same impulses. Initially, for Marcher they both exemplify love, hope, and life, even though at this early point he remains blind and insensible to external reality, but finally they represent despair, death, and loneliness, and at this stage the hero slowly achieves insight into his existence and realizes where he has failed. Mortality intrudes on his hallucinatory expectations and shows that the only way to escape anonymity and annihilation is through love and empathy. Thus, Marcher will spend his remaining years trying to win back the "lost stuff of consciousness": he becomes a prisoner of the past.

Even after her death, Marcher still considers May an extension of his being, for when he returns from his global travels, he hastens to her grave, "into his own presence": "he had been separated so long from the part of himself that alone he now valued." Although he now openly affirms his love for her, he still refuses to accept her individuality, for he is preoccupied by his own plight and by the impossibility of having his being validated by her recognition of his desires; he is impotent—a nonentity without her. Near her grave he feels most alive, for he realizes that

> the open page was the tomb of his friend, and *there* were the
> facts of the past, there the truth of his life, there the backward

> reaches in which he could lose himself. . . . he seemed to wander
> through the old years with his hand in the arm of a companion
> who was, in the most extraordinary manner, his other, his
> younger self; and to wander, which was more extraordinary
> yet, round and round a third presence—not wandering she, but
> stationary, still, whose eyes, turning with his revolution, never
> ceased to follow him, and whose seat was his point, so to speak,
> of orientation. Thus in short he settled to live—feeding only on
> the sense that he once *had* lived, and dependent on it not only for
> a support but for an identity.

Without May, he has no future or hope. The present offers him virtually no social identity, for he cannot even be publicly regarded as the bereaved husband. The objectification of his anxiety in the other, in the above passage, puts his mind at rest and allows him to escape the actuality of death by his immersion in the past.

But the final realization comes when he confronts another mourner at the cemetery, who shows the ravages of pain and loss at a beloved's grave. This man is representative of that other person Marcher might have been if he had not rejected May's love and had been willing to experience life. Although at first unable to understand this man's uncontrollable sorrow that contorts his physical expression, Marcher, through his projection onto this synchronic, alternate other, is permitted the cathartic release of emotion that he has long suppressed. At first, he wonders what made this stranger "so bleed and yet live," but then he realizes that this man reflects a state of being that May predicted Marcher would never know directly— the feeling of love or grief that he can experience only vicariously through another. And this lack is responsible for the hero's "arid end":

> No passion had ever touched him. . . . he had survived and
> maundered and pined, but where had been *his* deep ravage? . . .
> Now that the illumination had begun, however, it blazed to the
> zenith, and what he presently stood there gazing at was the
> sounded void of his life. . . . *she* was what he had missed. This
> was the awful thought, the answer to all the past. . . . he had
> been the man of his time, *the* man, to whom nothing on earth
> was to have happened.

He knows she had offered him the chance to have lived and loved, as she had, but he realizes that his egotism had prevented this from happening:

he had never thought of her . . . but in the chill of his egotism
and the light of her use. . . . This horror of waking—*this* was
knowledge. . . . belated and bitter, had something of the taste of
life. . . . He saw the Jungle of his life and saw the lurking Beast;
then, while he looked, perceived it, as by a stir of the air, rise,
huge and hideous, for the leap that was to settle him.

He now perceives her as an individual who had feelings and desires, but he
realizes his selfishness has blinded him to everything but his own needs.
Death, "huge and hideous," is awaiting Marcher, and, apprehending this,
he turns to the past for comfort. At the end, he attempts a synthesis of the
past, present, and future in that he establishes a continuity with what has
occurred and yet a recognition of inevitable death. Throughout, May functions as the mediator between reality and phantasy, and Marcher perceives
himself through her eyes, which is what gives him validity in the world.
Only at the end does the overwhelming epiphany occur, and he sees the
futility and barrenness of his life, caused by his egotism and blindness. The
beast and May, as the incarnations of the other, represent in either abstract
or concrete form Marcher's unconscious, unacknowledged sexual desire
and need to be loved, as well as his eventual disillusionment with a prospective, transforming experience and his ultimate confrontation with and
movement toward death.

In his manipulation and examination of the beast, Marcher, unable to
delimit the nature of its signification, represses and narrowly circumscribes
its meaning in that he refuses to acknowledge its sexual connotations. He
bars the signified and instead is in the clutches of a fetish. When he at last
comprehends the import of the beast, any satisfaction he might experience
concerning the successful completion of this analytic, reading process—
that is, the message contained in the symbol of the beast—is frustrated by
the tragic loss of May. Although there is an appropriation of meaning on
his part, this realization culminates in a tenacious grasp of death, in the
possession of a simulacrum, an image of reality. Here, as with the narrator
in *The Sacred Fount*, Marcher's attempt to master signification, to eliminate
contradiction and ambiguity is accomplished only through the infliction of
a mortal wound to May that brings about the irreversible distance and
separation between them, for in a sense he murders her since he denies the
existence of her desire and love (as well as his own repressed feelings).

Marcher's seizure of the beast, the signifier, thus creates an unrecover-
able, irreparable loss, for in his endeavor to capture the definitive interpretation, he encounters only death. In trying to erase his awareness of her

love and in professing ignorance of her intimations, he only brings about her final disillusionment and despair. To kill the ambiguity, the alternate and threatening possibilities inherent in the beast, would signify a mastery of meaning and also a suppression of sexual desire, but for Marcher this ultimately does not happen since May's death awakens him to the other significations contained in the metaphoric beast—love and passional fulfillment. Earlier, he wishes to blind himself to the truth of his impotence, and this conscious mastery results in the imposition of unification and homogeneity on the beast, in that he sees it as something wonderful that will happen to him, but something that excludes love, which is too mundane a solution for him. His demand of May for the definitive answer to the nature of the great event he is to experience reveals his desire not for the truth but for something that reflects his egotistical and grandiose phantasies. Thus, the signified, the actuality of love, is contained in the beast and in May, but Marcher refuses to recognize in the signifier the repressed, unconscious truth until it is much too late.

In "The Beast in the Jungle," there is aesthetic distance from and a spatialized representation of time, whose passage is perceived all at once from a privileged position. Although the story is concerned with the psychological description of Marcher's thoughts and reactions, the narrator's critical, moral, and controlling voice is still felt. Therefore, the points of view of the character and the narrator frequently do not concur. The irony is not as overt and biting as in *What Maisie Knew*, but it expresses the more knowledgeable perception of someone who has possibly experienced a similar withdrawal from and blindness to the world. The narrator's more encompassing and spatialized vision can be understood if one considers the roles of both the protagonist and his confidante. Marcher is the central consciousness, but May's tacit point of view seems to pervade the entire story. Through her, the irony of Marcher's aspirations is revealed. Her perspective is tinged with the narrator's knowledge of the hero, but it lacks his sometimes sarcastic tone and unsympathetic perception in that she perceives Marcher's egotism yet does not wish to hurt her friend and instead indulges him, hoping that a glimmering of the truth may come to him. Marcher's reservations about selfishly imposing himself on her are particularly ironic in view of the narrator's portrayal of his active exploitation of her, which perhaps is most fully exposed in Marcher's excuse for not marrying May: calling himself a "man of feeling," he has the idea that he cannot share his great adventure with a woman. Even in the sections of meditation, one senses the narrator's critical and privileged presence commenting on the hero's blindness. The analytical discussions he has with

May grow out of his solipsistic ratiocinations and amorphous proleptic deliberations and also reveal May's point of view, which functions as ironic commentary on his perceptions presented in the meditative parts of the narrative. Her role is in a way equivalent to the narrator's, for she sees the truth and attempts to educate him. Because of the use of much condensation, the iterative mode, and narrated discourse and a modicum of psychological expansion, free indirect style and immediate speech (internal monologue), the narrator's voice seems to dominate.

Although many years pass during the course of the story, nothing much appears to happen, and the slow and repetitious rhythm reinforces the aura of the futility and emptiness of Marcher's life. The hypothetical anticipations are vague and undelineated throughout the story and lose their force after May's death, at which point the repetitive retrospections become the dominant anachronism employed, reflecting Marcher's desire to recapture the past and his dismissal of an empty present and future. Even in the dramatic scenes between May and Marcher, where one has a better sense of the amount of historical time elapsing, one still has the feeling that they represent iterative occurrences, events that recur through the years and differ from one another primarily in minor details. Only the final chapter contains a scene of psychological description in which historical time approximates narrative time. Involving Marcher's epiphanic recognition of his loss, the language here is closest to the unmediated functioning of the mind. Generally, however, though condensed or isochronic psychological description predominates, the language manifests a controlling, ironic consciousness behind the text. Since Marcher rarely indulges in extrapolations or speculations about the content of the future, the present, or the past, there is little psychological expansion. One does not get lost in the living present of constantly multiplying possibilities, as, for example, in *The Ambassadors*, or even more noticeably in *The Sense of the Past*. The narrator retains his status as an "objective" observer of a sealed-off, formalized world, and he and the character do not progress together in discovering the meaning of the narrative world. Because of the narrator's distance from Marcher, there is a spatialized representation of time, for the objective voice visualizes the action and passage of time simultaneously from a privileged position.

As mentioned earlier, Marcher's life is initially predicated on the priority of the future, but, ironically, he is not actively involved in determining it. Although this anticipatory stance presents him with options, he makes no effort to select certain alternatives. He allows experience to act upon him and sits passively, awaiting the spring of the formidable beast.

Knowledge of any situation requires a temporal and imaginative synthesis which, in the consideration of a possible future, examines the relevant past in constructing the character of presentness and which bases the man of action, cognition, and moral decision in the world. However, Marcher, as suggested earlier, for most of his life rejects the past and present as possessing any significance and instead lives in the anticipation of the future, for he contemplates an abstract and vague conception of an imminent, transforming event, but he makes no effort either to select from the presentational field certain alternatives or finally to actualize this vision of specific potentialities in a concrete form. He refuses to make the "nothingness" of the future into a viable possibility through which to direct his actions. The only suggestion of temporal synthesis he achieves is at the end of the story when he turns toward the past for an explanation of his empty present. At this point, Marcher realizes that his inertia and failure to live a full life have somehow been predicated on his rejection of temporality. When his world disintegrates with the death of May, he experiences a rupture of the familiar reference points in his life, and therefore turns to the past in order to interpret the significance of his present. Now the future remains ominously void of meaning: it portends only delusion and death. Although his final recognition of his mortality makes him aware of his limitations, Marcher's realization is a passive understanding: he moves from ignorance to knowledge, but never from passivity to activity, and remains an observer of his own deadness and apathy. He does not make an active decision to come to terms with his past by integrating it within his present and instead immerses himself in it. Finally, he appropriates and captures the "lost stuff of consciousness," but this gesture is as futile as his fixation on the future: it also represents an abrogation of the will and a refusal to live.

Consequently, the recognition of the inevitability of death and the immersion in a past of "positing" presentification, rather than a concern with a vague and phantasmal future, represent Marcher's avoidance of present activity and significant involvement with his world. The belief in the suppositional future is therefore rejected in favor of an equally life-denying pursuit of an accomplished past and the possibilities in it that he eschewed. This becomes the case with many of James's middle-aged heroes in that they ignore the challenging and uncertain aspects of the future and the present and instead immerse themselves in the contemplation of a static and less threatening real or hypothetical past.

Marcher's anxiety about the future is not objectified, for he simply refers to it analogically as a beast waiting to pounce. It symbolizes not only his conscious anticipation of some amorphous, transfiguring experience but also his unconscious desires and fears. Marcher's being-for-others is narcissistic: an aspect of himself exists in May's consciousness, and this is what preserves and reinforces his identity and goals. Like all the female confidantes in the late works, May represents his alter ego, the external validation of his phantasies, yet she also embodies his subliminal need to be loved; but Marcher refuses to recognize in her the concrete possibility of a transmuting love and passion and instead prefers to live in expectation of some great impalpable event. With the metamorphosis of the beast from an image of hope to one of despair, as symbolized by May's parallel transformation and death, he faces his own finiteness and extinction. Confronting the emptiness of the future, he turns to the memories of the past for vicarious fulfillment.

In . . . works discussed [elsewhere] there is progressive objectification and materialization of the individual's anxiety, reflecting the Jamesian character's growing fear of the present and inability to live fully in his contemporary situation. The hero, in these circumstances, superimposes his unconscious desires upon the external world in the form of a conflict between self and other. The future as hopeful and viable is rejected. Instead, the character turns to the past or to a hypothetical present for an interpretation of the significance of his existence and projects his anxiety upon the other in order to avoid the threatening reality of a future that contains not only physical death but the further destruction of an aesthetic and moral way of life that he finds obsolete in the modern world.

In . . . other late works . . . there is the need to "resee" the past in the light of the present, to relive it through an act of memory, or to compose a phantasmal past or hypothetical present that reflects inner desires, whereas in "The Beast in the Jungle" the hero tends to nullify this past and lives in expectation of some transforming future event. Thus, while the characters in the later works live in a universe juxtaposing the past and the present, Marcher initially inhabits a world in which the former is shunned but is found to be ultimately inescapable, and in which the latter is only the transitional stage, the means to an end, for the future is the goal of the hero who constantly lives beyond himself and the actual moment. Only the humiliating knowledge that May had understood the nature of the great experience and that it had already occurred turns his life into an "arid desert" of retrospective regrets, and the futural beast of death is ready to pounce. Marcher has perverted the whole thrust of his existence. In all the works James wrote after "The Beast in the Jungle," the character no longer looks to prospective possibilities in a world he feels he cannot control. Instead, he accepts the future as empty and turns to both the actual and the hypothetical past and present in order to recapitulate lost potentialities and to explore the viability of alternate selves.

Since the Imaginary cannot accommodate death, its plenitude must resist that traumatic moment in which, confronted with lack and difference, the individual recognizes that the existence of the world is not dependent on his creative vision. Thus, James's hero sees the future as a void, containing only death; in order to fill this vacuum and escape the implications of mortality, he looks to the past for fulfillment, for he attempts to reestablish the origins of the self and to bring it into present significance. For a specific working out of such possibilities, he investigates and immerses himself in "the sense of the past" and in an examination of alternate states of being that result in the phenomenological exercise that James outlines in [certain] late short stories, unfinished novels, and "autobiographical" works.

"Hanging Fire": The Primal Scene of *The Turn of the Screw*

Ned Lukacher

An obscure revelation of a referentiality that no longer refers to anything more than the evidentiality of an event that is no longer an event.

JACQUES DERRIDA, *"Préjugés"*

Of the critics of Henry James's *The Turn of the Screw*, Shoshana Felman writes: "In repeating as they do the primal scene of the text's meaning as division, the critics can by no means master or exhaust the very meaning of that division, but only act the division out, perform it, be part of it." Here indeed is a text whose "polytonality" cannot be mastered. Like the governess herself, the critic is thwarted whenever he or she tries to grasp the real and tries to wrest from the unmasterable tone of *The Turn of the Screw* a determinant or univocal meaning. At every "turn" James invites his readers to make a construction and to attempt a solution. But as Felman's essay "Turning the Screw of Interpretation" definitively establishes, there is simply no way to avoid repeating the text's fundamental division between the uncanny ghostliness of the governess's visions and the hysterical mechanisms that inform them.

The point I would like to make here, however, does not directly concern the difference between the psychic and the sexual. While Felman is quite right to demonstrate how James implicates the reader in every effort by the governess to construct the primal scene, and to demonstrate that the governess's dilemma as analyst is that of every reader, she does not pose the question of the precise nature of the governess's constructions. It is

From *Primal Scenes: Literature, Philosophy, Psychoanalysis.* © 1986 by Cornell University. Cornell University Press, 1986.

one thing to say that, try as they may, critics can never demystify the governess's mystification and are condemned to repeat it; it is quite another thing to say, as I shall, that James's interest is as much in the specific nature of the governess's process of construction as it is in the indeterminacy of the finished product. What neither Felman nor any other critic of *The Turn of the Screw* has analyzed is the specificity of the governess's visions/hallucinations. Numerous details and many of the most extraordinary scenes in the story have gone unnoticed, or at least unexplained, because the critical focus has been on the governess's state of mind rather than on the particularity of the vision in question.

I want to make it clear, however, that without Felman's innovative reexamination of the controversy surrounding this text, I would never have been led to the reading that follows. Once again, the Heideggerian principle that errancy is not simply nontruth but rather the primordial "counteressence" of truth has enabled me to recognize that the governess's errancy preserves traces of the truth of the events at Bly House. The Heideggerian-Derridean position with respect to the truth is not a pluralistic one. Though interpretation is a nonfinite process, this is not to say that all interpretations are equally valid, or that they are indeterminate in quite the same way. Interpretation is open-ended because interpretation is a kind of "remembering," a "remembering" that has been made possible by a particular temporal conjunction. Interpretation is a kind of "remembering" which, in the process of recovering what has been forgotten, keeps itself open to subsequent "memories" in the future. It is this aspect of interpretation that Heidegger suggests by the word *andenken* or "commemorative thinking," a remembrance that turns forward, toward thinking, *andenken*, in the very act of turning back. From where we are now, a "new" reading of *The Turn of the Screw* is possible—or more precisely, a "commemoration" of what has been forgotten in the text, a "commemoration" of the text's most fundamental level of concealment-disclosure. Without Felman's work, I would not have been able to "remember" what has been "forgotten" by the text and its critics for almost a century.

The critical history of *The Turn of the Screw* reveals that there has been more interest in James's figure of the analyst than in the constructions she makes. Like the critics Freud describes in *From the History of an Infantile Neurosis*, who believe that the fact that the analyst proposes the primal scene and the patient does not remember it decides the whole question, critics of James's text have focused so myopically on either the hysterical projections of the governess or the possibility of psychic phenomena that they never consider the fundamental question posed by Freud's construction of the primal scene: What is the relation of the phantasy to reality? Without forgetting that the real remains out of our grasp, I will attempt here to relate the governess's constructions to the analyst's construction of the primal scene, to determine what primal scene or *fabula* lies behind the *sjuzet* that is her narrative. Her narrative, like the wolf dream, contains within itself a *fabula* that, while not constituting the real, nevertheless brings us closer to it than we could otherwise reach.

The question, therefore, is not whether the governess's visions involve sex or the supernatural but whether they compose an account of the events prior to her arrival at Bly House which, though still concealing the real, at least approximates it. In effect we are shifting what Felman calls "the text's meaning as division" from the *sjuzet* to the *fabula*. Through her visions the governess is trying to remember something that everyone else is trying to forget. But like an intemperate analyst, she comes to believe too vehemently in her own constructions of an event that remains rigorously unknowable. Because of the extent of her mystification, critics have focused solely upon her inability to distinguish reality from phantasy but have forgotten to consider the possibility that those phantasies are nevertheless related to the real. Even Felman, in the course of her otherwise brilliant Lacanian reading of the story, has omitted all reference to the real, which is a profoundly non-Lacanian reading strategy. The concealment of the real and one's inability to grasp it are never for Lacan reasons to forget the real. The critics of *The Turn of the Screw* have forgotten the story's temporality, which is the pathway to the real. Only by reconstructing that temporality will we be able to move beyond mere indeterminacy. Like the ghosts of ontotheology, the ghosts of Peter Quint and Miss Jessel pose the question of the origin through the medium of the question of time. James's "tone" is an achievement that must be placed in conjunction with the Freudo-Heideggerian notion of the temporality of the non-originary "event."

"In so far as the analyst is supposed to know," writes Lacan, "he is also supposed to set out in search of unconscious desire." The governess errs in setting out on this search with perhaps a little too much determination, though we might as easily say too much self-righteousness or prurience: "What it was least possible to get rid of was the cruel idea that, whatever I had seen, Miles and Flora saw more —things more terrible and unguessable and that sprang from dreadful passages of intercourse in the past." While an analyst would be concerned with the neuroses that might have developed in the children as a result of having witnessed the primal scene, the governess is concerned that the spectacle of *coitus flagrante* has placed the children within the diabolical power of the returning spirits of

Quint and Jessel. (As we will see, for the governess the primal scene is literally a *flagrant* spectacle in the etymological sense of the word *flagrante*, "blazing.") Though these "things" are still "unguessable" at this early point in the text, the governess will soon be making quite a few guesses, which Freud would call "suppositions" (*Annahmen*). Like the analyst, the governess cannot expect corroboration except for an occasional slip of the tongue from Mrs. Grose. Finally, like an analyst who succeeds only in driving the patient away, the governess will lapse from this salutary skepticism with regard to the limits of her knowledge into a grotesque certitude that will no longer admit any interdictions barring the way to the primal scene.

Suddenly confronted, in broad daylight, with the vision of the ghost of Miss Jessel at the writing desk—which reminds us that in this story the primal scene is always one of writing—the governess tries to grasp the vision in its entirety, to take it all in, only to discover that "even as I fixed and, for memory, secured it, the awful image passed away." "Fixing" her gaze and "securing" an image in her memory are emblematic of the governess's behavior. Convinced that the children, whether unconsciously or not, have been "fixed," or rather fixated, upon the primal scene, the governess turns all her attention to their fixation, which in turn becomes her fixation and thus that of the reader. In the following passage James goes out of his way to fix our attention on "fixing." Mrs. Grose and the governess are discussing Miss Jessel:

> Mrs. Grose, at this, fixed her eyes a minute on the ground; then at last raising them, "Tell me how you know," she said.
> "Then you admit it's what she was?" I cried.
> "Tell me how you know," my friend simply repeated.
> "Know? By seeing her! By the way she looked."
> "At you, do you mean—so wickedly?"
> "Dear me, no—I could have borne that. She gave me never a glance. She only fixed the child."
> Mrs. Grose tried to see it. "Fixed her?"
> "Ah with such awful eyes!"

Mrs. Grose's response to this report of Jessel's "awful eyes" renders this scene a repetition and displacement of the very scene it describes: "She stared at mine as if they might really have resembled them." Mrs. Grose sees in the governess what the governess sees in her vision of Miss Jessel. She sees the same "fury of intention" and the same desire "to get hold of" the children. In Jessel's desire to possess the souls of the children, the governess sees her own desire to seize upon the children's unconscious desire.

This is indeed an allegory of the analyst's desire to know. It is the task of the Jamesian "tone" to mark the diacritical point where analysis becomes a kind of possession.

No less than Freud, James too was "fixed," captivated by the voice of the hysterical woman. In a regrettably ignored article, Oscar Cargill suggests that *The Turn of the Screw* is a response to the ideas, if not the text, of Freud's *Studies on Hysteria* and to the mental illness of James's sister, Alice. In "The New York Preface" to the story, James describes his effort as that of catching "those not easily caught . . . the jaded, the disillusioned, the fastidious": that is, those who are not fooled by the supernatural trappings and who recognize that the governess's visions are the result of hysterical repression. Such readers *will* be "caught" if they assume that simply because the governess is phantasizing, her visions have no relation to reality. As Felman demonstrates, nothing could be further from the Jamesian "tone" than a reductive psychoanalytic reading. From his brother William, and from the family's experience with mental disorder, Henry recognized that psychological analysis was situated somewhere between a reductive literality and an ambiguous figurality—which is to say that the Jamesian "tone" is situated somewhere between the philosophical truth and the literary lie. It is situated in the psychoanalytic space that Freud and Lacan carved out between philosophy and literature. Felman, however, allows herself to be "caught" by identifying the Jamesian "tone" with the power of the literary and the figural: "In inviting, in seducing the psychoanalyst, in tempting him into the quicksand of its rhetoric, literature, in truth, only invites him to subvert himself, only lures psychoanalysis into its necessary self-subversion." Felman's "in truth" indicates how securely she has been "fixed" by the Jamesian "tone." Were what Felman says here true, James would be simply a run-of-the-mill modernist. But *The Turn of the Screw* does not stage some putative overcoming of philosophy by literature, any more than it stages the overcoming of literature by analysis. James and Freud and Lacan are more radical than Felman implies, for what they stage is nothing less than the primal scene of philosophy, literature, psychoanalysis. *The Turn of the Screw* subverts those analysts who think of themselves as ontologists. But what Felman forgets is that James's story also subverts those analysts who believe they have overcome ontology thanks to something called "literature." James makes a more profound demand on our notion of reading than Felman or her mentor, Paul de Man, seems willing to admit. The "disillusioned" reader who believes that everything is "literature" believes that everything is demystified insofar as everything is a mystification. Such a reader, standing at the "end" of metaphysics and in possession of "the truth," forgets that fundamental concealments persist. Such a reader believes that we have finished with the ghosts of ontotheology. James recognized, however—and he remains our contemporary because of this recognition—that we have not finished with these ghosts, and that the relation between phantasy and reality, though unreadable, continues to make its uncanny call upon our imaginations. James seems implicitly to have realized that deconstruction is neither an anti-ontology nor a post-ontology but a pre-ontology.

Felman, no less than the governess, renders analysis a kind of possession by privileging the figurality of the "literary." A more attentive reading —one that does not, however, go so far as to be "fastidious"—can still discern the erased trace of the real within the governess's phantasies. The achievement of the Jamesian "tone" is that it grants ontological primacy to neither reality nor language, to neither the literal nor the figural. It "fixes" us in the space where it itself is "fixed," in the space of the preontological, the ghostly space at the beginning of the end of metaphysics.

Miss Jessel is at the heart of the governess's construction of the primal scene. From Mrs. Grose she learns that Miss Jessel became pregnant with Quint's child and was sent home, where she presumably died, as the result of either a miscarriage or an abortion: "She couldn't have stayed. Fancy it here—for a governess! And afterwards I imagined—and I still imagine. And what I imagine is dreadful." These revelations by Mrs. Grose enable the governess to rationalize her strange predisposition to despise her precursor. Her aggressive detestation of a woman she has never met is one of the most disturbing features of her illness. She even speaks, again by way of rationalization, of the ability of women to "read one another." Her propensity to believe the worst of Miss Jessel is in marked contrast to Douglas's characterization of Jessel in the prologue to the story as "a most respectable person":

> So far had Douglas presented his picture when someone put a question. "And what did the former governess die of? Of so much respectability?"
>
> Our friend's answer was prompt, "That will come out. I don't anticipate."
>
> "Pardon me—I thought that was just what you are doing."

Is Douglas misleading us in the very act of letting us in on the secret? If he is not, then he is undermining one of the governess's major themes and in effect suggesting that her bitter recriminations against Miss Jessel are utterly delusional. Clearly, he is anticipating, despite his disclaimer. But that still does not make us any more or less certain of the reliability of his assurances of Jessel's respectability. Here indeed is an exemplary instance of the Jamesian "tone" at work: it directs us to a particular problematic at the same time that it calls into question both its own reliability and the significance of the very thing toward which it turns our attention. It is precisely by virtue of the hermeneutic interference it generates that the Jamesian "tone" calls attention to itself. James questions Miss Jessel's respectability by first establishing that this is a question that can never be resolved, a question whose answer will remain concealed, a question that both must be and cannot be answered.

"Was there a 'secret' at Bly—a mystery of Udolpho or an insane, an unmentionable relative kept in unsuspected confinement?" The governess's question poses an interesting critical question about the relation between the reader of the Gothic novel and the psychoanalyst who constructs a primal scene. Is it because Ann Radcliffe and Charlotte Brontë construct their romances around a woman's unhappy fate that the governess's interest is so riveted on Miss Jessel? James certainly does seem to be suggesting something of the kind. The governess's mind is full of Gothic stereotypes. In her visions of Miss Jessel, James presents a series of vignettes that recall the consummate villainess of Victorian melodrama, Lydia Gwilt, the anti-heroine of Wilkie Collins's very successful *Armadale* (1866). No less than those of Swinburne or William Morris, Collins's heroines have often grotesquely fetishized tresses, which are always most striking against a mourning gown. Behind the governess's vision of her predecessor in the schoolroom, James's readers would doubtless have thought first of the fiery-haired Miss Gwilt, in mourning, furiously penning her interminable diary.

Unlike James, however, the Gothic tradition from Radcliffe to Collins often seems oblivious to its most glaring contradictions. As always, the effect of stereotype and cliché is to displace attention from contradictions. As readers of *The Mysteries of Udolpho*, for example, we suspect throughout that the heroine is in fact the daughter of an incestuous relation and that all her travails are the effects of an unforgiving God who punishes the children for the sins of the fathers. But Radcliffe hasn't the heart to pursue the question she herself has posed, and we never learn why Emily's father regarded the picture of his sister with such special affection. The Gothic text demands that we construct a primal scene but thwarts our ability to carry through with the effort. Likewise, in *Jane Eyre* we have no idea why Rochester keeps his mad wife in the attic of his main estate rather than on a neighboring estate he also owns. Rochester had claimed that it was unhealthy to live on his second estate but forgets those reservations when, after the fire, he and Jane move there. We are never let into the secret for this particular confinement, just as we never learn how Jane could have heard that mysterious, telepathic voice that marks the climactic point of the novel. The Gothic novel opens the space for the construction of the primal scene and in the same gesture bars access to it.

But in James's story, the governess's madness is, at its most elemental level, a refusal to be barred from learning the "secret": that is, a refusal to forget ontology. It is in order to continue her pursuit of the secret that she produces her visions. Her visions are like analytic constructions, for through each one she is able to sound out Mrs. Grose more fully. The old lady is particularly struck by one detail in the governess's account of her first vision of Jessel's ghost. Through his punctuation of the governess's account, James lets us observe her hesitant, piecemeal method of construction: "In mourning—rather poor, almost shabby. But—yes—with extraordinary beauty." To which Mrs. Grose responds: "The person was in black, you say?" Though this is not at all a verification of her observation, the governess, as is her habit, jumps to conclusions and interprets Mrs. Grose's curiosity about Jessel's mourning dress as an indication that she is really on to something here: "I now recognized to what I had at last, stroke by stroke, brought the victim of my confidence, for she quite visibly weighed this."

Who is the "victim" here? Is it really Mrs. Grose? Quite to the contrary, the governess is victimizing herself. She is the victim of her own intemperate desire to get to the bottom of it all. Mrs. Grose has no reason whatsoever to associate Jessel with mourning attire; she is struck by this detail because it does *not* fit in place. But the governess sees only what she wants to see, and so she reads the old lady's response as confirmation that she is on the right track. A screenplay would note that Mrs. Grose poses her question—"The person was in black, you say?"—with a quizzical tone of surprise. It is precisely this diacritical mark at the level of tone that the governess is unable to read. There is indeed a track here, but she errs in thinking that she is on the right one. The task of reading James is one of remembering that although there is a right track, we are not going to be on it.

The first question, therefore, is why the governess dresses Miss Jessel in mourning. Is it simply her predilection for the Gothic? In part, yes, but there is something more at stake here. The governess is so taken with her apparent success that she employs this detail again in her highly dramatic vision of Jessel in the schoolroom. The apparition at the writing desk is "dark as midnight in her black dress, her haggard beauty and her unutterable woe." As the governess enters the room, she imagines that the figure at the desk might be a "housemaid" who "had applied herself to the considerable effort of a letter to her sweetheart." The entire scene is the very epitome of Gothic melodrama: the vision of a beautiful, distraught ghost of a woman in mourning as she rises in an eloquently silent gesture of despair. The tone here is also the epitome of James:

> Then it was—with the very act of its announcing itself—that her identity flared up in a change of posture. She rose, not as if she had heard me, but with an indescribable melancholy of indifference and detachment, and, within a dozen feet of me, stood there as my vile predecessor. Dishonored and tragic, she was all before me; but even as I fixed and, for memory, secured it, the awful image passed away.

"With the very act of its announcing itself." What indeed is "announcing itself" in this scene? What does the governess mean by "her identity flared up"? And why the strange construction, "stood there as my vile predecessor," rather than the simpler and anticipated "stood there my vile predecessor"? Every effect of James's carefully crafted tone here creates an ambivalence between self and other. What is *not* announced here is the "identity" of the ghost, or even its identity *as* a ghost. What is announced is the clearly self-reflexive nature of the governess's imagination.

For whom is Jessel in mourning, and to whom is she writing? If she is mourning for Quint, then she surely would not be writing to him. The governess has only recently learned of Quint's death at the time of this vision, and it is quite natural for her to assume that the lascivious Jessel is in mourning for her lover; however, such a scenario is contradicted by the chronology Mrs. Grose sets forth. The question then is, What kind of events do the visions represent? As far as I can determine, all of the governess's visions take place in the present. They are not glimpses into the past but events of a present haunting. Why, then, should Jessel be in mourning, since Quint is also on the premises? And to whom could she be writing? One might respond that supernatural visitations do not have to have a logic and to look for one is misguided. But if that is the case, why does James take pains to establish a chronology of the events preceding the governess's arrival at Bly if he does not intend that chronology to serve as a cipher against which to read the legitimacy of the governess's visions? Only by taking these details into account can we reconstruct the temporality of the story.

As we shall see, James's chronology makes it quite clear that Jessel could never have been in the schoolroom in mourning for Quint. Further-more, we know that when she has this vision, the governess is intending to write a letter to the master, in violation of his mysterious interdiction against such correspondence. This interdiction against writing, which is indeed the ultimate gesture of an authoritarian metaphysics and which the critics have never explained, looms large in my reading of the story. What, then, are we to make of the governess's figure of the "housemaid" about to write a letter to her "sweetheart"? What is "announcing itself" is the constructive power of the governess's unconscious phantasy. But beyond this obvious point lies the question of the relation of that phantasy to the actual events concerning the two ill-fated servants. Though her phantasy is merely an image or a figure of the real, it is only in relation to that un-reality that we are able to deduce a relation to the real. The ghost at the writing desk is a figure for both Miss Jessel and the governess herself.

The art of James's tone is that it conceals within the governess's self-mystification an effort to demystify the secret at Bly. James situates us between the supernatural reading that would insist that this is a psychic phenomenon and the psychological reading that would insist that this is simply a hysterical self-projection. For the governess is really not so mad at all, and the supernatural is really no less uncanny for being a synthesis of the real and the phantasized. We must always remember that James is demystifying not only the supernatural but also our presuppositions about mental disorder. We must always remember to displace both sets of pre-suppositions when reading *The Turn of the Screw*. Though her phantasy is in error, it forcefully announces the need to construct a more lucid account of the prehistory of this present haunting.

Let us now reconstruct the chronology. The governess arrives in June. Mrs. Grose has had the care of Flora for several months already, and Miles is about to return from school for the summer: hence the pressing need for a new governess. We know from Mrs. Grose that the pregnant Miss Jessel left Bly "at the end of the year," and that by the time she was expected back after the holidays, news came from the master that she had died. This means that she died sometime during the winter. Miss Jessel, already—to Mrs. Grose at any rate—noticeably pregnant, left Bly in December only to die at home some weeks later.

Early in the story, at the point where the governess is questioning the housekeeper about the man she saw on the tower, Mrs. Grose explains that Quint and the master

> "were both here—last year. Then the master went, and Quint was alone."

I followed, but halting a little. "Alone?"

"Alone with *us*." Then as from a deeper depth, "In charge," she added.

The italicized *us* and the suggestion of "a deeper depth" imply that this was the period of the primal scene. The children were there, Miss Jessel was there, and Quint was "in charge." Everything is in place, even the chronology, for we are now in the summer, which must have been the time when Jessel became pregnant if her condition was noticeable by December. The master's departure has serious consequences as far as Mrs. Grose is concerned; she is implying that had Quint not been left in charge, the children's otherwise "respectable" governess would never have succumbed, as she did, to a "fellow" whom Mrs. Grose calls "a hound." This is made clear much later in the text when the governess suggests that the master is to blame.

"After all," I said, "it's their uncle's fault. If he left here such people —!"

"He didn't really in the least know them. The fault's mine." She had turned quite pale.

Here the governess has indeed hit the mark, but this time she doesn't even recognize it. Clearly, Mrs. Grose agrees with what is for the governess only an offhand remark. But what is it that makes her turn "quite pale"? Surely mere negligence on the master's part would not have been enough. No, James is trying to tell us something more; we have reached the "deeper depth" that the governess sensed was at stake. Mrs. Grose knows that it was the master's fault but not because of his negligence or inattention. She tells the governess that "the master believed in [Quint] and placed him here because he was supposed not to be quite in health and the country air so good for him. So he had everything to say." Reading James closely enough to know how to read him freely enough reveals that what makes Mrs. Grose turn so pale is her awareness that the master did know what he was doing when he left Quint in charge, that he knew Quint well enough to know what effect the man would have on the otherwise "respectable" Miss Jessel.

James has set forth not only a chronology of the events of the preceding summer, though one does have to read between the lines to construct it, but also an etiology of the primal scene itself. We know from the prologue what a playboy the master is and what an effect he has upon our governess, the narrator. If even Mrs. Grose knew that Quint was "a hound," then we can be certain that the master recognized those same instincts in this favored employee, who even has the privilege of wearing the master's clothes. We know, even though the governess never pursues it beyond her passing remark to Mrs. Grose, that the master is deeply culpable in this scandalous affair. Like the governess, the critics have been blind to the artful Jamesian tone that informs Mrs. Grose's speech and gesture. It is for that reason that none of them has ever remotely guessed why the master absolutely forbids his servants to write to him. It is the most appallingly obvious thing that critics always miss. As any reader of Lacan's seminar on Poe's "Purloined Letter" might have recognized, the master is in the place of the real. In *The Turn of the Screw* it is not the letter but the absence of the letter that enables us to trace the path of the signifier to the real. But like Poe, James can only point to the real without explicating it. We never know what is in the letter the Minister D— has stolen, and we never know why the master staged the primal scene at Bly. Like a Joycean god, he remains far behind the scenes, paring his fingernails while, unseen, he directs the action. The secret of the primal scene at Bly is finally in his nature, and that nature James keeps securely out of reach.

In sketching the chronology, we have inquired into the etiology of the primal scene. We must still, however, return to the question of mourning and death. We know that Miss Jessel died during the winter, sometime between December and March. Only the master knows the exact date. We know that Quint too died over that same winter. Coming home from the village, no doubt drunk as would befit such a debauchee, he slipped on the ice, hit his head, and died. In other words, Quint and Jessel died at roughly the same time, which means that she could never have been in mourning for him at Bly. Furthermore, she probably would not have mourned his death in any case. Miss Jessel, if I am reading James correctly, is a respectable woman who was seduced and became pregnant with tragic results— the furthest thing from the stormy, romantic heroine the governess makes her out to be. *The Turn of the Screw* is really a pathetic tragedy of a woman caught in the machinations of a decadent patriarchy.

The story is much more sordid and commonplace than the governess would have wanted to admit. She fills every detail with all sorts of Gothic paraphernalia, whereas, like the mystery of the master's interdiction forbidding correspondence, what lies behind the vision in the schoolroom is only a tawdry Victorian tale of the suffering of an innocent woman. The master forbids his servants to write for the very simple reason that he wants nothing more to do with Bly or the children. He has sense enough to recognize the havoc his involvement has brought on and wisely decides to forgo any further involvement in the lives of his servants. He simply wants to cover his tracks and pretend that the whole thing never happened. But something did happen, and Mrs. Grose does not dare let on for fear of losing her job. Only the governess dares to guess at the "unguessable." Her constructions, regardless of the personal investment she has made in them, are always moving toward the rediscovery of that something. And it is only through her constructions that we are able to find our way to the primal scene of the story.

In "The New York Preface" to *The Turn of the Screw*, James describes his achievement in terms of a tone that seems a precursor to Derrida's "apocalyptic tone": "The study is of a conceived 'tone,' the tone of suspected and felt trouble, of an inordinate and incalculable sore — the tone of tragic, yet of exquisite, mystification." Notice the care with which James calculates the effect of the "incalculable." On the one hand there is the tone of suspicion, the tone that speaks of "an inordinate and incalculable sore"; on the other hand there is a tone of tragic mystification. In other words, the event remains "incalculable" because it can only be approached in terms of a mystified tone. The governess's tragic airs, her lurid Gothic imagination, become for James a synecdoche for the work of unconscious phantasy in general, which is always already at work in the determination of an event. The construction I have made here concerning the master and Quint, and my unraveling of the governess's visions, remain tentative efforts to calculate the "incalculable." Nothing in James's text or letters, or from any other source, will verify them absolutely. What I have constructed is the primal scene of *The Turn of the Screw*, and it is situated, as James made certain it would be, in the zone of *différance*, in that complex temporal space of the always already but not yet. It is an origin that is an effect of its effects. It is not real, but it takes us closer to the real than any other reading has done. Far from extinguishing the "incalculable," the construction of the primal scene opens a new path toward it. In making such a construction we do not dispel the ghosts; to the contrary, we ensure that they live on behind an ineradicable concealment. As the ciphers of an "incalculable sore," the ghosts can never be done away with, for they are the figures of the challenge and necessity of reading. To rest at the level of indeterminacy is to forget that "sore" and to fall victim once again to the ruses of male power.

Like "The Purloined Letter," *The Turn of the Screw* is mediated by a complex narrative frame. The governess writes her manuscript at an unspecified date, and then sends it to Douglas before she dies. Douglas, in turn, reads it at the Christmas gathering and then, before his death, has it sent to his host, who recopies the manuscript and has it published. With each link in the chain of transmission, James is at once establishing the nonoriginary in the place of the origin and focusing our attention on the question of the origin. By presenting his text as a veritable palimpsest of a multiple scene of writing, each layer of which distances us from the voice of the governess, James at once discloses and conceals the question of the origin.

What I want to turn to now is the role that metaphor plays in *The Turn of the Screw* in revealing and concealing the question of the origin. More particularly, I want to look at the image of fire as a metaphor of the origin. In its self-consuming play of absence and presence, fire perfectly suits the demand that the Jamesian tone makes upon language.

The governess writes of the ghost in the schoolroom that its "identity flared up in a change of posture." At the most expressive moment of its anguish, the ghost appears to burst into flame, to consume itself, and disappear. In a later scene, while on the grounds of the estate with Mrs. Grose, the governess frantically tries to point out to her companion the "hideous" figure of Miss Jessel, who she insists is standing directly in front of them:

> "You don't see her exactly as we see?—you mean to say you don't see now—*now*? She's as big as a blazing fire! Only look, dearest woman, *look*—!"

The old lady responds in a manner that anticipates those critics whose focus is exclusively on the errors of "literature": "It's all a mere mistake and a worry and a joke." This is indeed the response of the "fastidious" reader, the one who reads so closely as to be myopic. Of course, the difference here is that Mrs. Grose, unlike the fastidious reader, knows that there is something behind this sheet of flame, even though she would rather turn her glance away. For the governess, the figure of fire is a most appropriate one to describe the demonic forces she has set out to vanquish. Though she is steadfast in her struggle against evil, she must sometimes remind herself that "it was not my mere infernal imagination." Between her and the secret knowledge that she believes the children possess, there always looms the disfiguring figure of fire. If she could only see through, or beyond it, she would truly grasp the truth. But as soon as it flares up, as if in a moment of apocalyptic revelation, it invariably vanishes into thin air.

Fire in *The Turn of the Screw*, writes Shoshana Felman, "consumes, incinerates at once the content of the story and the inside of the letter, making both indeed impossible to read, unreadable, but unreadable in such a way as to hold all the more 'breathless' the readers' circle round it." Felman is referring to Miles's incineration of the governess's prohibited letter to the master, and to the guests gathered round the fireside to hear Douglas read the manuscript. The figure of fire does, as Felman suggests, "eliminate the center," but it does not, for all that, leave us only with emptiness and the loss of the center. It seems to me that on precisely this question we can distinguish the position of Freud, Heidegger, Nietzsche, or Derrida from that of the "Yale School" of deconstruction. In one of his early essays Derrida characterizes Nietzschean affirmation as that which *"determines the noncenter otherwise than as loss of the center."* In other words, even with the loss of the possibility of a determinable origin, there is a kind of gain. Something that is neither presence nor absence persists even in the loss of the origin, and it is to this something that Nietzsche responds with his "immense, unbounded Yes." Felman's notion of unreadability stops short of Derridean *différance*. The figure of fire does not simply destroy the center; it also *"determines the noncenter otherwise than as loss of the center."* At the beginning of her discussion of fire, Felman cites a passage from Lacan that makes the Heideggerian-Derridean point wonderfully clear: "We do not see what is burning, for the flame blinds us to the fact that the fire catches on the real." Everything depends upon our remembering that even though the fire blinds us to the real, we have not forgotten that the real, as the indeterminable noncenter, is there as something other than an absence.

In a footnote to this citation from Lacan, Felman writes of "the crucial importance of fire in Henry James's life, and its recurrent role, both real and symbolic, as a castrating agent." Fire played a tragic role in James's own life and in that of his father. The fact that James's father lost a leg as the result of a fire and that in another incident James himself suffered a permanent back injury forcefully suggests why fire had such an important role to play in manifesting the real as a mode of concealment and withdrawal. In James's texts, fire brings the real to presence only by staging its concealment and withdrawal. James uses fire to blind us to the real, but we should not be blinded to the fact that the real is still there to be blinded to. The French psychoanalyst Jean Laplanche has argued that fire is the paradigmatic figure for the perception of the traumatic event. In James's life and art, this seems indeed to be the case.

There is in the later James a phrase that appears so insistently that one might, at the risk of a slight exaggeration, regard it as a tic, or compulsive element, in the late Jamesian tone. In his texts of the 1890s, above all in *The Turn of the Screw* and *The Wings of the Dove*, James uses the expression "hanging fire" in a variety of permutations and in conjunction with a wide spectrum of character and situation. Regardless of age, social class, or sex, everyone in the latter James seems capable of "hanging fire." Without reservation we can say that this expression is synonymous with the incalculability of the later Jamesian tone. "To hang fire" means "to hesitate," "to remain concealed," "to withdraw, or step back, in the very act of seemingly stepping forward to say something." "To hang fire" is "to keep something hidden in the very act of apparently revealing something." By noting the point at which someone "hangs fire," James locates the point of maximum resistance, the point at which saying something also becomes a way of not saying something else. Felman never mentions the expression and even elides it when it appears in a passage she is citing. Yet she is well aware of the principle that is at stake here: "Mrs. Grose," Felman writes, "in saying less than all, nonetheless says more than she intends to say."

And it is in connection with Mrs. Grose that James repeatedly uses the phrase. The governess remarks of the old lady, "She hung fire, but she overcame her reluctance." In response to her inquiries about the man on the tower, Mrs. Grose "hung fire so long that I was still mystified." "Hanging fire" describes the structure of communication throughout *The Turn of the Screw*, and it is no exaggeration to say that it could easily have been the story's alternate title. "Hanging fire" describes the same "turn" away from determinable meaning which we come to expect at each of the numerous "turns" in the story. "Hanging fire" is synonymous with the hesitation waltz of Jamesian tone.

The expression, from the early history of firearms, describes any discernible delay between the ignition of the powder and the actual firing of the ball. "To hang fire" is thus to be on the threshold between firing and not firing, in the interval between speech and silence. This may well have been a common phrase among the country gentry of James's acquaintance; wherever he learned it, it must have seemed to him made to order to describe the play of concealment and disclosure. In Douglas's evasion of his audience's queries in the story's prologue, and especially when his host asks him to begin, we might see an image of James himself. As Douglas turns away from his interlocutors, he turns "round to the fire," which he watches for an instant before facing his audience once again. In this alternating rhythm of turning toward and then away from the fire, we enter the primal scene of the Jamesian text.

Chronology

1843	Born April 15 in New York City.
1862	Enters Harvard Law School.
1864	First story, "A Tragedy of Error," published (unsigned).
1865	First signed tale, "The Story of a Year," published.
1869–70	Grand tour of Europe. Meets George Eliot, William Morris, D. G. Rossetti, Darwin, and Ruskin, among others.
1871	First novel, *Watch and Ward*, published serially.
1875	*A Passionate Pilgrim and Other Tales*, first book, published.
1878	"Daisy Miller" published, to great acclaim. Begins living in Europe.
1881	Returns to America for a year.
1882	Mother and father die.
1884	"The Art of Fiction" published.
1888	*The Aspern Papers*, and other collections of tales, published.
1889	*A London Life*, including "The Liar," published.
1891	*The American* produced as a play in London.
1892	*The Lesson of the Master*, collection of tales, published.
1893	*The Real Thing and Other Tales* published.
1895	Failure of play *Guy Domville*. *Terminations*, including "The Altar of the Dead," published.
1896	*Embarrassments*, including "The Figure in the Carpet," published.
1897	Begins dictating all written work.
1898	*The Turn of the Screw* and "In the Cage" published.
1904	Returns to the United States again.
1905	American lecture tour; returns to England and begins revisions for "New York Edition" of collected works.
1906	"The Jolly Corner" published.

1907	Publication of New York Edition begins, ultimately includes 24 volumes and 18 prefaces.
1911	Receives honorary degree from Harvard University.
1913	First volume of autobiography published.
1914	Involved in war relief activities.
1915	Becomes a British citizen.
1916	Dies February 28 in London.

Contributors

HAROLD BLOOM, Sterling Professor of the Humanities at Yale University, is the author of *The Anxiety of Influence, Poetry and Repression*, and many other volumes of literary criticism. His forthcoming study, *Freud: Transference and Authority*, attempts a full-scale reading of all Freud's major writings. A MacArthur Prize Fellow, he is general editor of five series of literary criticism published by Chelsea House. During 1987–88, he was appointed Charles Eliot Norton Professor of Poetry at Harvard University.

LAURENCE HOLLAND taught English at Princeton University and The Johns Hopkins University. He has written *The Expense of Vision*, co-authored *The Literary Heritage of New Jersey*, and edited *Who Designs America?*.

CAROL OHMANN teaches English at Wesleyan University.

WOLFGANG ISER teaches English and Comparative Literature at the Universität Konstanz in Germany and the University of California, Irvine. A pioneer of "reception aesthetics" criticism and a founder of the "Poetics and Hermeneutics" research group, he has written books on Fielding, Pater, Spenser, and Beckett as well as *The Act of Reading, The Implied Reader*, and *Der Appelstruktur der Texte*.

MOSHE RON teaches English and Comparative Literature at the Hebrew University in Jerusalem. He has published articles on James's "The Liar" and free indirect discourse.

J. HILLIS MILLER teaches English and Comparative Literature at the University of California, Irvine. He has taught previously at The Johns Hopkins University and Yale University. President of the Modern Language Association for 1986, he has written books on Dickens and Hardy as well as *The Disappearance of God* and *The Forms of Victorian Fiction*. His most recent books are *Fiction and Repetition, The Linguistic Moment*, and *The Ethics of Reading*.

135

Deborah Esch is Andrew W. Mellon Assistant Professor of English at Princeton University. She is the author of *The Senses of the Past: The Rhetoric of Temporality in Henry James* as well as articles on Benjamin, Kant, Hume, Woolf, Wordsworth, Kleist, Shelley, and Paul de Man. She is co-editing two collections of essays by Jacques Derrida, *The Institutions of Philosophy* and *Negotiations*.

Donna Przybylowicz teaches English at the University of Minnesota, Twin Cities. She is editor of the journal *Cultural Critique* and has published a book on James called *Desire and Repression: The Dialectic of Self and Other in the Late Works of Henry James*.

Ned Lukacher teaches the history of literary criticism in the Department of English at the University of Illinois, Chicago. He is the author of *Primal Scenes: Literature, Philosophy, Psychoanalysis* (1986) and has translated two French books on Freud and psychoanalysis.

Bibliography

Auchard, John. "The Scent of Decadence: The Ghostly Tales." In *Silence in Henry James*, 31–53. University Park: Pennsylvania State University Press, 1986.

Banta, Martha. *Henry James and the Occult*. Bloomington: Indiana University Press, 1972.

Barnett, Louise K. "Jamesian Feminism: Women in 'Daisy Miller.'" *Studies in Short Fiction* 16 (1979): 281–87.

Bell, Ian F. A., ed. *Henry James: Fiction as History*. London: Vision Press Ltd., 1984.

Bersani, Leo. "The Jamesian Lie." In *A Future for Astyanax: Character and Desire in Literature*, 126–55. Boston: Little, Brown, 1976.

Bewley, Marius. *The Complex Fate*. London: Chatto & Windus, 1952.

Blackmur, R. P. "In the Country of the Blue." In *Studies in Henry James*, edited with an introduction by Veronica A. Makowsky, 69–90. New York: New Directions, 1983.

Blake, Nancy. "Le regard de l'autre: double ou imposture." In *Le double dans le Romanticisme anglo-américain*, edited by Christian La Cassagnère. Clermont-Ferrand: Faculté des Lettres et Sciences Humaines de l'Université Clermont-Ferrand, 1984: 179–89.

Blanchot, Maurice. "The Turn of the Screw." In *The Sirens' Song*, translated by Sacha Rabinovitch, 79–86. Bloomington: Indiana University Press, 1982.

Bosanquet, Theodora. *Henry James at Work*. London: Hogarth, 1924.

Brooke-Rose, Christine. "The pure fantastic: types of analysis." In *A Rhetoric of the Unreal*, 103–229. Cambridge: Cambridge University Press, 1981.

Buitenhuis, Peter. *The Grasping Imagination*. Toronto: University of Toronto Press, 1970.

Caws, Mary Ann. "High Modernist Framing: Framing in the Later James." In *Reading Frames in Modern Fiction*, 121–206. Princeton: Princeton University Press, 1985.

Chambers, Ross. "Not for the Vulgar?: The Question of Readership in 'The Figure in the Carpet.'" In *Story and Situation*, 151–80. Minneapolis: University of Minnesota Press, 1984.

Chatman, Seymour. *The Later Style of Henry James*. New York: Barnes & Noble, 1972.

Cixous, Hélène. "Henry James: L'Écriture comme placement ou de l'ambiguité de l'intérêt." *Poétique* 1 (1970): 35–50.

Clair, John A. *The Ironic Dimension in the Fiction of Henry James*. Pittsburgh: Duquesne University Press, 1965.

Donadio, Stephen. *Nietzsche, Henry James, and the Artistic Will*. New York: Oxford University Press, 1978.

Dupee, Frederick W. *Henry James*. New York: Sloane, 1951.

———, ed. *The Question of Henry James: A Collection of Critical Essays*. New York: H. Holt & Co., 1945.

Eaton, Marcia. "James' Turn of the Speech-Act." *British Journal of Aesthetics* 23, no. 4 (1983): 333–45.

Edel, Leon, ed. *The Complete Tales of Henry James*. 12 vols. London: R. Hart-Davis, 1962–64.

———. *Henry James*. 5 vols. Philadelphia: Lippincott, 1953–72.

———, ed. *Henry James: A Collection of Critical Essays*. Englewood Cliffs, N.J.: Prentice-Hall, 1963.

Felman, Shoshana. *Writing and Madness*. Ithaca: Cornell University Press, 1985.

Ford, Ford Madox. *Henry James*. London: Martin Secker, 1913.

Fowler, Virginia. "The Psychology of the International Drama and the Requirements of its Heroine." In *Henry James's American Girl*, 29–40. Madison: University of Wisconsin Press, 1984.

Freundlieb, Dieter. "Explaining Interpretation: The Case of Henry James' 'The Turn of the Screw.'" *Poetics Today* 5, no. 1 (1984): 79–95.

Gale, Robert L. *The Caught Image: Figurative Language in the Fiction of Henry James*. Chapel Hill: University of North Carolina Press, 1964.

Henry James. Special issue of *L'arc* 89 (1983).

———. Special issue of *Hound and Horn* 7, no. 3 (April–May 1934).

Henry James Review. November 1979–present. Journal of the Henry James Society, published at the Department of English, Louisiana State University, Baton Rouge.

Holland, Laurence Bedwell. *The Expense of Vision: Essays on the Craft of Henry James*. Rev. ed. Baltimore: Johns Hopkins University Press, 1982.

Kappeler, Susanne. *Writing and Reading in Henry James*. New York: Columbia University Press, 1980.

Kaston, Carren O. "In the Cage." In *Imagination and Desire in the Novels of Henry James*, 108–20. New Brunswick: Rutgers University Press, 1984.

Kimbrough, Robert, ed. *"The Turn of the Screw"*. Norton critical edition. New York: Norton, 1966.

Kraft, James. *The Early Tales of Henry James*. Carbondale: Southern Illinois University Press, 1969.

Krook, Dorothea. "The Turn of the Screw" and "The Beef and the Little Tarts." In *The Ordeal of Consciousness in Henry James*. 106–34, 325–54. Cambridge: Cambridge University Press, 1962.

Leavis, F. R. *The Great Tradition*. London: Chatto & Windus, 1948.

Lock, Peter W. "'The Figure in the Carpet': The Text as Riddle and Force." *Nineteenth-Century Fiction* 36 (1981): 157–75.

Lukacher, Ned. "'Hanging Fire': The Primal Scene of 'The Turn of the Screw.'" In *Primal Scenes: Literature, Philosophy, Psychoanalysis*, 115–32. Ithaca, N.Y.: Cornell University Press, 1986.

McKee, Patricia. *Heroic Committment in Richardson, Eliot and James*. Princeton: Princeton University Press, 1986.

Mackenzie, Manfred. *Communities of Honor and Love in Henry James*. Cambridge: Harvard University Press, 1976.

Matthiessen, F. O. *Henry James, The Major Phase*. New York: Oxford University Press, 1963.

Miller, J. Hillis. "A Guest in the House." *Poetics Today* 2, no. 1b (1980–81): 189–91.

Mull, Donald K. "The Early Tales." In *Henry James's "Sublime Economy"* 14–26. Middletown, Conn.: Wesleyan University Press, 1973.

Norman, Ralf. *The Insecure World of Henry James' Fiction: Intensity and Ambiguity.* New York: St. Martin's, 1982.

———. *Techniques of Ambiguity in the Fiction of Henry James.* Abo: Abo Akademi, 1977.

Perrot, Jean. *Henry James: une écriture enigmatique.* Paris: Aubier-Montaigne, 1982.

Poirier, Richard. *The Comic Sense of Henry James: A Study of the Early Novels.* New York: Oxford University Press, 1960.

Pontalis, J.-B. "Le Lecteur et son auteur: A propos de deux récits de Henry James." In *Après Freud,* 336–55. Paris: Gallimard, 1971.

Porter, Katherine Anne, Allen Tate, and Mark Van Doren. "James' 'The Turn of the Screw': A Radio Symposium." In *The New Invitation to Learning,* edited by Mark Van Doren, 223–35. New York: Random House, 1942.

Przybylowicz, Donna. *Desire and Repression: The Dialectic of Self and Other in the Late Works of Henry James.* University: University of Alabama Press, 1986.

Rimmon, Shlomith. *The Concept of Ambiguity—The Example of James.* Chicago: University of Chicago Press, 1977.

———. "Barthes' 'Hermenutic Code' and Henry James' Literary Detective." *Hebrew University Studies in Literature* 1, no. 2 (1973): 183–207.

Rimmon-Kenan, Shlomith. "Deconstructive Reflections on Deconstruction." *Poetics Today* 2, no. 1b (1980–81): 185–88.

Robbins, Bruce. "Shooting Off James's Blanks: Theory, Politics, and 'The Turn of the Screw.'" *Henry James Review* 5, no. 3 (1984): 192–99.

Ron, Moshe. "The Art of the Portrait according to James." *Yale French Studies* 69 (1985): 222–37.

Rowe, John Carlos. *Henry Adams and Henry James: The Emergence of Modern Consciousness.* Ithaca, N.Y.: Cornell University Press, 1976.

———. "Psychoanalytical Significances: The Use and Abuse of Uncertainty in 'The Turn of the Screw.'" In *The Theoretical Dimensions of Henry James,* 119–46. Madison: University of Wisconsin Press, 1984.

Salmon, Rachel. "Naming and Knowing in Henry James's 'The Beast in the Jungle.'" *Orbis Litterarum* 36 (1981): 302–22.

Samuels, Charles Thomas. *The Ambiguity of Henry James.* Urbana: University of Illinois Press, 1971.

Schor, Naomi. "Fiction as Interpretation/Interpretation as Fiction." In *The Reader in the Text,* edited by Susan R. Suleiman and Inge Crossman, 165–82. Princeton: Princeton University Press, 1980.

Shapland, Elizabeth. "Duration and Frequency: Prominent Aspects of Time in Henry James' 'The Beast in the Jungle.'" *Papers on Language and Literature* 17, no. 1 (1981): 33–47.

Segal, Ora. *The Lucid Reflector: The Observer in Henry James's Fiction.* New Haven: Yale University Press, 1969.

Siebers, Tobin. "Hesitation, History, and Reading: Henry James' 'The Turn of the Screw.'" *Texas Studies in Language and Literature* 25 (1983): 558–73.

Siegel, Eli. *James and the Children.* New York: Definition Press, 1969.

Sollers, Philippe. "Le secret." In *Logiques.* Paris: Editions du Seuil, 1968.

Springer, Mary Doyle. *A Rhetoric of Literary Character: Some Women of Henry James*. Chicago: University of Chicago Press, 1978.

Stafford, William T., ed. *James's "Daisy Miller": The Story, the Play, the Critics*. New York: Scribner's, 1963.

Sussman, Henry. "James: The Twists of the Governess." In *The Hegelian Aftermath*, 230–39. Baltimore: Johns Hopkins University Press, 1982.

Sweeney, Gerald. "The Deadly Figure in James' Carpet." *Modern Language Studies* 13, no. 4 (1983): 79–85.

Tanner, Tony. *Henry James*. Amherst: University of Massachusetts Press, 1985.

Telotte, J. P. "The Right Way with Reality: James' 'The Real Right Thing.'" *Henry James Review* 6, no. 4 (1984): 8–14.

Todorov, Tzvetan. "The Secret of Narrative." In *The Poetics of Prose* translated by Richard Howard, 143–78. Ithaca, N.Y.: Cornell University Press, 1977.

Tompkins, Jane P. "'The Beast in the Jungle': An Analysis of James' Late Style." *Modern Fiction Studies* 16 (1970): 185–91.

———, ed. *Twentieth-Century Interpretations of "The Turn of the Screw" and Other Tales*. Englewood Cliffs, N.J.: Prentice-Hall, 1970.

Vaid, Krishna Baldev. *Technique in the Tales of Henry James*. Cambridge: Harvard University Press, 1964.

Wagenknecht, Edward. *The Tales of Henry James*. New York: Ungar, 1984.

Wegelin, Christof, ed. *Tales of Henry James*. Norton critical edition. New York: Norton, 1984.

Willen, Gerald, ed. *A Casebook on Henry James' "The Turn of the Screw"*. 2d ed. New York: Crowell, 1969.

Yeazell, Ruth Bernard. *Language and Knowledge in the Late Novels of Henry James*. Chicago: University of Chicago Press, 1976.

Zéraffa, Michel, ed. *L'Art de la fiction, Henry James*. Paris: Éditions Klincksieck, 1978.

Acknowledgments

"The Aspern Papers" by Laurence B. Holland from *The Expense of Vision: Essays on the Craft of Henry James* by Laurence B. Holland, © 1964, 1982 by Faith Holland. Reprinted by permission of Faith M. Holland.

" 'Daisy Miller': A Study of Changing Intentions" by Carol Ohmann from *American Literature* 36, no. 1 (March 1964), © 1964 by Duke University Press. Reprinted by permission.

"Partial Art—Total Interpretation" (originally entitled "Partial Art—Total Interpretation: Henry James, "The Figure in the Carpet," In Place of an Introduction") by Wolfgang Iser from *The Act of Reading: A Theory of Aesthetic Response* by Wolfgang Iser, © 1978 by the Johns Hopkins University Press, Baltimore/London. Reprinted by permission.

"A Reading of 'The Real Thing' " by Moshe Ron from *Yale French Studies* no. 58 (1979), © 1979 by *Yale French Studies*. Reprinted by permission.

" 'The Figure in the Carpet' " by J. Hillis Miller from *Poetics Today* 1, no. 3 (Spring 1980), © 1980 by *Poetics Today*, The Porter Institute for Poetics and Semiotics, Tel Aviv University. Reprinted by permission.

"A Jamesian About-Face: Notes on 'The Jolly Corner' " by Deborah Esch from *ELH* 50, no. 3 (Fall 1983), © 1983 by the Johns Hopkins University Press, Baltimore/London, © 1985 by Deborah Esch. Reprinted by permission of the author and the Johns Hopkins University Press.

"The 'Lost Stuff of Consciousness': The Priority of Futurity and the Deferral of Desire in 'The Beast in the Jungle' " by Donna Przybylowicz from *Desire and Repression: The Dialectic of Self and Other in the Late Works of Henry James* by Donna Przybylowicz, © 1986 by the University of Alabama Press. Reprinted by permission.

" 'Hanging Fire': The Primal Scene of *The Turn of the Screw*" by Ned Lukacher from *Primal Scenes: Literature, Philosophy, Psychoanalysis* by Ned Lukacher, © 1986 by Cornell University. Reprinted by permission of Cornell University Press.

141

Index

Addard, C. P. ("Fordham Castle"). *See* Taker, Abel

Adventures of Huckleberry Finn, The (Clemens), 8, 10, 25

Alter, Robert, 66

Alter ego: confrontation with, 78, 81, 91; creation of, 82–83; description of, 88–89; disfigurement of, 89–90; as quarry, 80, 85–86; as symbol for figurative language, 77, 83–84, 91

Archer, Isabel (*The Portrait of a Lady*), 6

Armadale (Collins), 123

Artemisia ("The Real Thing"), 44

Artist: as agent of transformation, 44, 48; belittling of, 58; and model, 45, 50, 55; perversity of, 53; and social code, 51–52; unreliability of, 55–57

Aspern, Jeffrey ("The Aspern Papers"): as collaborator, 12–14; as opportunist, 21; as Orpheus, 14; power of, 19

"Aspern Papers, The": caricature in, 19–20; courtship in, 17–18; double perspective in, 11–23; drama in, 20–23; form of, 19, 22; historical uncertainty in, 15; Orpheus image in, 14–15, 17, 22, 23; reader as collaborator in, 12

Barthes, Roland, 59

Bartram, May ("The Beast in the Jungle"): as analyst, 102–3; and beast symbol, 102; death of, 94, 95, 98, 103, 104, 108; dehumanization of, 104–5; as embodiment of desire, 100–1; as Marcher's alter ego, 99–100, 105–6, 109–10, 115; as mediator of reality and fantasy, 111; and past, 107; point of view of, 112; as symbol of life, 109

"Beast in the Jungle, The": atmosphere of repression in, 103–4; beast symbol in, 98, 101–2, 105–6, 109, 111–12, 114; narrative voice in, 94, 112–13; past and future in, 93–116; representation of time in, 112, 113; "whistling in the dark" image in, 88

Blanchot, Maurice, 75

Bordereau, Juliana ("The Aspern Papers"), 11, 12, 13; betrayal of, 14; as Eurydice, 15; and marriage, 16–17; and money, 15–16; power of, 19

Bordereau, Tina ("The Aspern Papers"), 11, 12, 13; and drama, 21; liberation of, 19; and marriage, 16–17; transformation of, 18, 22–23

Brontë, Charlotte, 123–24

Brydon, Spencer ("The Jolly Corner"), 77; and amputation, 89; as figure for James, 78, 79; and literalization, 82–85; and metaphor, 87–88;

Brydon, Spencer *(continued)*
    obsession with past of, 81–82, 93;
    and personal vs. impersonal, 87;
    self-mystification of, 83–84;
    "turning" of, 79–80, 81; and
    unrealized possibilities, 76. *See also*
    Alter ego

Calvino, Italo, 76, 90
Cargill, Oscar, 121
Carlyle, Thomas, 38, 39
Cather, Willa, 1
Churm, Miss ("The Real Thing"), 46,
    57; flexibility of, 49–50, 53
Cixous, Hélène, 58
Clemens, Samuel, 8, 10, 25
Collins, Wilkie, 123
Corvick ("The Figure in the Carpet"),
    36, 39, 40, 41, 71, 72
Corvick, Gwendolen, 39, 41–42, 71, 72
Costello, Mrs. ("Daisy Miller"), 27–28
Crane, Stephen, 25
Critic ("The Figure in the Carpet").
    See Narrator ("The Figure in the
    Carpet")
Croy, Kate (*The Wings of the Dove*), 85

"Daisy Miller": change of attitude in,
    26–34; controversial character of,
    25; Europe vs. America in, 26–30,
    33; limitations of, 30–31, 32–33,
    34; nationalism in, 2; nature in,
    31–33, 34; New York edition of,
    33–34
Daisy Miller ("Daisy Miller"). *See*
    Miller, Daisy
Deane, Drayton, 39, 71, 72
de Man, Paul, 54, 121
Dencombe ("The Middle Years"), 75
Densher (*The Wings of the Dove*), 85
Derrida, Jacques, 59–60, 131
de Vionnet, Mme. (*The Ambassadors*),
    106
Douglas (*The Turn of the Screw*), 122–23,
    129, 131

du Maurier, George, 44, 57–58
Dunbar, Viola R., 33–34
Dupee, F. W., 25–26

Eliot, T. S., 3
Emerson, Ralph Waldo, 1, 2–7, 10
Empson, William, 67
Erme, Gwendolen ("The Figure in the
    Carpet"), 71
Eurydice, 15, 23
"Experience" (Emerson), 7

Faulkner, William, 1
Felman, Shoshana, 117, 118, 119, 121,
    122, 130–31, 132
"Figure in the Carpet, The": catachre-
    sis in, 70; comedy in, 68, 69, 71;
    detachment of reader in, 39–40,
    42; interpersonal relationships in,
    71; search for meaning in, 69–70;
    secret in, 71–72; sexual knowledge
    in, 72; subject-object interaction
    in, 41; and textual interpretation,
    35–42; title of, 40; unreadability
    of, 66–67, 68, 69
Finn, Huck (*The Adventures of Huckle-
    berry Finn*), 25
Fleming, Henry (*The Red Badge of
    Courage*), 25
Flora (*The Turn of the Screw*), 119–20
Fontainier, Pierre, 83
Freud, Sigmund, 118, 121, 131
Friedman, Alan, 66
From the History of an Infantile Neurosis
    (Freud), 118

Garrett, Peter, 66
Giovanelli ("Daisy Miller"), 28, 29, 30,
    33; and natural world, 31, 32
Goddard, Harold, 9
Gostrey, Maria (*The Ambassadors*), 106
Governess (*The Turn of the Screw*): as
    analyst, 117, 118, 119, 120–21; and
    fire metaphor, 130; fixation of,

120; hallucinations of, 117–18, 119; and melodrama, 123, 124–25, 128; and Miss Jessel, 122; self-reflexive fantasies of, 125, 126; as victim, 124

Gray (*The Ivory Tower*), 98

Grose, Mrs. (*The Turn of the Screw*), 120, 122, 124; and fire metaphor, 130, 132; and guilt of master, 127–28, 129

Gwilt, Lydia (*Armadale*), 123

Hague, Acton ("The Altar of the Dead"), 107

Hartman, Geoffrey, 59

Hassan, Ihab, 25

Hawley ("The Real Thing"), 50, 58, 59

Hawthorne, Nathaniel, 1

Heidegger, Johann, 97, 118, 131

Hero-Worship (Carlyle), 38

Interpretation: appearance in, 38, 50–51; and error, 118; function of, 37–39; historical norms in, 35, 37; imagistic meaning in, 40–41; problem of, 43; as remembering, 118; search for meaning in, 39, 40, 66–68, 69–70; and subject-object interaction, 41; and unreadability, 66–68, 69; violence of, 36–37, 55

Jakobson, Roman, 51

James, Alice, 121

James, Henry: and American myth, 34; on character, 49; on continuity, 61–62, 63, 64–65; on "Daisy Miller," 33; and Emerson, 2–7, 10; as expatriate, 1–2, 6; and Faulkner, 1; and Hawthorne, 1; influences on, 1–7; and interpretation, 38; on "The Real Thing," 44–45; return to America of, 77–78; and Twain, 8, 10. *Works:* "The Altar of the Dead," 107; *The Ambassadors*, 2, 88, 106, 113; *The American*, 2; *The American Scene*, 6–7, 77; *The Awkward Age*, 7; "The Bench of Desolation," 106; *The Bostonians*, 7; "Crapy Cornelia," 93, 99; "Fordham Castle," 95–97; "Friend of Friends," 107; *The Golden Bowl*, 65; *The Ivory Tower*, 98; "Maud-Evelyn," 107; "The Middle Years," 75; "New York Revisited," 77, 89; Notebooks, 44, 45, 52, 78–79; "Owen Wingrave," 106; *Partial Portraits*, 19; "The Passionate Pilgrim," 78; *The Portrait of a Lady*, 6, 45; "Preface to *Roderick Hudson*," 61–62, 72–73; "Preface to *The Golden Bowl*, 86; "Preface to the New York Edition," 7–8, 33, 121, 129; "Preface to *The Turn of the Screw*," 121, 129; *The Princess Casamassima*, 7; "The Pupil," 7–10; "A Round of Visits," 93, 99; *The Sacred Fount*, 98, 99, 102, 105, 111; *The Sense of the Past*, 78–79, 93, 113; *A Small Boy and Others*, 79; *The Spoils of Poynton*, 7; *What Maisie Knew*, 7, 8, 112; *The Wings of the Dove*, 85, 131

James, Henry Sr., 2

James, William, 7, 121

James' fiction: aesthetic theory in criticism of, 48; ambiguity in, 67; anxiety in, 115; catachresis in, 65–66; economic exchange in, 52; economy of representation in, 43; fear of sexuality in, 108; figure as flower in, 65–66; focus vs. length in, 65; future as empty in, 115–16; "hanging fire" image in, 131–32; littleness as symbol in, 58; loss of capacity for love in, 28; metaphor in, 77; moral life in, 6; past in, 93, 114; quotation marks in, 80; subjects of, 54–55; tone of, 121, 122, 123, 132; unrealized possibilities in, 75, 95; women in, 99, 106–8, 115

Jane Eyre (Brontë), 123–24

Jessel, Miss (*The Turn of the Screw*), 119–20, 124–25; respectability of, 122–23; as tragic figure, 128

"Jolly Corner, The,": alternate readings of, 76–77; autobiographical basis of, 77; catachresis in, 85; dream in, 90–91; as examination of figurative language, 75–91; first-person narration in, 80–81, 84; hunting analogy in, 80, 85–86; literalization in, 82–85; metaphor in, 77; past in, 93; prosopopoeia in, 83, 85, 87; revisions of, 77; subordination of woman in, 99; "turning the tables" image in, 79–80, 86; uncertainty in, 88

Juliana Bordereau ("The Aspern Papers"). *See* Bordereau, Juliana

Kermode, Frank, 66
King Lear (Shakespeare), 9

"La Double Séance" (Derrida), 59–60
Lacan, Jacques, 121, 128, 131
Laplanche, Jean, 131
Les figures du discours (Fontanier), 83
Levin, Harry, 75
Lost Lady, A (Cather), 1

Magaw, Mrs. ("Fordham Castle"), 95–97, 106
Marcher, John ("The Beast in the Jungle"): catharsis of, 110; and death, 94, 95, 98, 103, 108–9, 114; deformation of reality of, 106; denial of sexuality of, 100–1, 105; fixation on future of, 93, 114, 115; insight of, 95, 108–9, 110–11, 112; isolation of, 94, 95; loss of social identity of, 95, 110; and May Bartram, 98–100, 101–2, 104–5; narcissism of, 99, 102, 105–6, 109, 115; passivity of, 97–98, 103, 113–14; and past, 95, 107, 109–10,

111, 114; search for meaning of, 102–3
Marmaduke ("Maud-Evelyn"), 107
Master (*The Turn of the Screw*), 127–29
Miles (*The Turn of the Screw*), 119–20, 130–31
Miller, Daisy ("Daisy Miller"): as American, 27–28; death of, 30–31; idealization of, 33–34; innocence of, 25–26; limitations of, 29–30; and natural world, 31–33, 34; sympathy with, 28, 29
Miller, Mrs. ("Daisy Miller"), 30
Monarchs ("The Real Thing"), 45; appearance of, 50–51, 52; as aristocrats, 57; as imitators, 60; limitations of, 50; marriage of, 57; and master-slave polarity, 46–47; name of, 51; narrator's interpretation of, 55–57; as obstacle, 44, 45; power of, 59; reality of, 47–48, 56–57; and reversal, 49; as signifier, 54
Monteith, Mark ("A Round of Visits"), 93
Morgan ("The Pupil"), 8–10
Muldoon, Mrs. ("The Jolly Corner"), 90
Mysteries of Udolpho, The (Radcliffe), 123

"Narrative Irony in Henry James' 'The Real Thing'" (Toor), 55
Narrator ("The Aspern Papers"): awakening to love of, 18, 23; duplicity of, 11–12; guilt of, 19, 20; and marriage, 17, 22; and money, 16; and Orpheus image, 14, 17; as poet, 13, 14; retreat of, 21; unreliability of, 15
Narrator ("The Figure in the Carpet"): failure of, 39; impotence of, 72; obtuseness of, 70; resistance of reader to, 35, 39–40; search for meaning of, 36, 37, 69, 70–71
Narrator ("The Real Thing"). *See* Artist ("The Real Thing")

Newsome, Mrs. (*The Ambassadors*), 106
Nietzsche, Friedrich, 3, 131
Novelist: and boundaries, 61–63; and
    continuity, 61–62, 63, 64–65; as
    embroiderer, 62, 63–64, 65–66,
    73–74; as father, 73; self-reflection
    of, 66

On Racine (Barthes), 59
Oronte ("The Real Thing"), 46, 47, 50
Orpheus, 14–15, 17, 22, 23

Pasquale ("The Aspern Papers"), 17
Pemberton ("The Pupil"), 8–9
Pendrel, Ralph (*The Sense of the Past*), 93
Poe, Edgar Allan, 128, 129
"Poems of Our Climate, The"
    (Stevens), 2
Poulet, Georges, 59
Power of Blackness, The (Levin), 75
Prest, Mrs. ("The Aspern Papers"), 11,
    17, 19; as collaborator, 12
"Purloined Letter, The" (Poe), 128, 129

Quint, Peter (*The Turn of the Screw*),
    119–20, 125, 128

Radcliffe, Ann, 123
Radical Innocence (Hassan), 25
Ramsay, Rutland ("The Real Thing"),
    44, 54
Randolph ("Daisy Miller"), 27
"Real Thing, The," 43–60; aesthetic
    theory in, 48–49; chiasmus in, 43,
    54, 58–59; demystification in,
    45–46, 50, 51, 60; mimesis in, 59–
    60; Oedipal complex in, 57–58, 59;
    polarities in, 44, 45, 46–47, 48, 60;
    social code in, 52–53; studio
    system in, 44, 45; symmetry in, 46,
    47, 53, 58–59; unreliable narrator
    in, 55–57; vocabulary of coercion
    in, 49, 55

Red Badge of Courage, The (Crane), 25
Rimmon, Schlomith, 66–67

Sand, George, 15, 16
Searle, Clement ("The Passionate
    Pilgrim"), 78
Sexuality: denial of, 100–1, 105, 111–
    12; fear of, 108; and knowledge,
    72
Shakespeare, William, 9
Staverton, Alice ("The Jolly Corner"),
    81–82, 84, 85, 91–92
Stevens, Wallace, 2
Stransom ("The Altar of the Dead"),
    107
Strether, Lambert (*The Ambassadors*), 7,
    106–7
Studies on Hysteria (Freud), 121

Taker, Abel ("Fordham Castle"),
    95–97, 98, 106
Taker, Sue ("Fordham Castle"), 96
Theale, Milly (*The Wings of the Dove*),
    85
Tina, Miss ("The Aspern Papers"). *See*
    Bordereau, Tina
Toor, David, 55
Turn of the Screw, The: chronology in,
    125–27; criticism of, 117, 118–19,
    128; fire metaphor in, 130–32;
    mental illness in, 121, 126; mystifi-
    cation in, 117–18, 129; narrative
    frame of, 129–30; primal scene
    in, 117–32; reader's response to,
    130; truth in, 119, 121–22; writing
    as symbol in, 120, 126
"Turning the Screw of Interpretation"
    (Felman), 117
Twain, Mark. *See* Clemens, Samuel

Vanderplank, Mrs. ("Fordham
    Castle"). *See* Magaw, Mrs.
Vereker ("The Figure in the Carpet"),
    36, 37, 38, 39, 40, 41; male

Vereker (*continued*)
  chauvinism of, 71; and search for
  meaning, 68–69, 70
Vereker, Mrs. ("The Figure in the
  Carpet"), 71–72

Walker, Mrs. ("Daisy Miller"), 28, 30
Wharton, Edith, 1

White-Mason ("Crapy Cornelia"), 93
Whitman, Walt, 1
Winterbourne, Frederick ("Daisy
  Miller"), 31, 33; Europeanization
  of, 27; rigidity of, 28–29

Yeats, William Butler, 6, 9